EAT
DRINK
SHINE

EAT
DRINK
SHINE

INSPIRATION FROM OUR KITCHEN

GLUTEN-FREE AND PALEO-FRIENDLY RECIPES

JENNIFER, JESSICA, & JILL EMICH

KYLE BOOKS

To all who will read this book,
may it serve you well.

To all who helped shape this book,
may we continue to inspire one another.

And to each other, may our sisterhood continue
to give us the courage, the reflection
and the unconditional love to dive deep
and live beyond our wildest dreams.

First published in Great Britain in 2016 by
Kyle Books, an imprint of Kyle Cathie Ltd
192–198 Vauxhall Bridge Road
London SW1V 1DX
general.enquiries@kylebooks.com
www.kylebooks.co.uk

10 9 8 7 6 5 4 3 2 1

ISBN 978 0 85783 325 9
Text © 2016 by Jennifer Emich, Jessica Emich and Jill Emich
Design © 2016 Kyle Books
Photographs © 2016 Eva Kolenko *
* except pages 8, 10, 16–17, 50, 88, 119, 120–121 and author photos on cover
© 2016 Cary Jobe Photography
and restaurant photo on page 185 © 2016 OmLight Photography

Project Editor: Jessica Goodman

Copy Editor: Sarah Scheffel

Angliciser: Lee Faber

Designer: Mark Latter

Photographer: Eva Kolenko

Food Stylist: Jeffrey Larsen

Prop Stylist: Natasha Kolenko

Production: Nic Jones, Gemma John and Lisa Pinnell
Colour reproduction by f1 colour

Printed and bound in China by 1010 International Printing Ltd.

CONTENTS

FOREWORD

I met Jessica, Jill and Jennifer many years ago, while I was living in Costa Rica. Fresh out of high school and feeling unsure of what I wanted to do with my life, I decided to spend a few months travelling around Central America. Ten days into my trip I made it to Dominical, a sleepy surf town on the Pacific coast of the country. I fell madly in love with the place and, not having any responsibilities in life aside from making sure I didn't misplace my backpack, I decided to stay. I spent my first year immersing myself in the world of wellness. I started practising yoga every day and would wake up at sunrise to meditate on the beach and then roll out my mat in one of the lifeguard towers, saluting the sun as it rose out of the jungle behind me. When I heard of a yoga retreat taking place in town, I decided to ask if I could join in. Jessica, Jill and Jennifer, or the Blissful Sisters from Boulder as they were called, had teamed up with Wade Imre Morisette to lead a week-long retreat right around the corner from my house. This was the very beginning of my yoga practice and, never having taken part in a retreat before, I was unsure of what to expect. One of my earliest memories of my yoga practice is practising with the triplets, being guided into Ardha Chandrasana and falling over, while Jennifer was solid as a rock. I was filled with awe by her groundedness and calm and thought to myself; 'one day I'll be that grounded, too.'

The next day the sisters guided us through the world of food and nutrition. Having gone through so many changes in such a short time during my travels, my life was like a blank page. What did I want to fill my days with? What kind of patterns should I stick to when it came to my diet, and what should I drop? The sisters taught me so much about the connection between my wellbeing and the things I chose to fuel my body with throughout the day. This was the first time I had spent time contemplating the importance of eating real, whole foods from the earth. I was amazed by how different I felt when I chose to actually listen to my body. That one retreat with the Blissful Sisters was the beginning of a completely new life for me, a life where yoga, meditation and nutritious foods together would become the foundation on which I built my life. It would still be years before I started teaching yoga, and I had no idea what life had in store for me at the time. Not in my wildest dreams could I have imagined that I would go on to lead my own retreats, write a *New York Times* bestseller, and dedicate my life to guiding people toward a balanced life in the future.

I am so grateful for having met Jessica, Jill and Jennifer at the very beginning of my journey, and I know you are going to love this book just as much as I do. May it bring you lots of joy, nourishment and inspiration in the kitchen!

Much love,

Rachel Brathen

Yoga Girl

OUR STORY

Life is all about practice, trial, error, successes and opportunities for growth. You never get to where you are going without first having to experience the journey, the wrong turns, the side paths and the beautiful horizons. This book is not about preaching that there's one way, it's not saying that how we choose to live is the only way. We are all constantly working on ourselves. We are here to ask only one thing, that you aspire to create a relationship with your body through your food, to understand it, to be at peace with your body and to (dare we say it!) LOVE it. This comes from one thing and one thing only, learning to listen deeply to it. Not because of what someone tells you is right or wrong, but because it is your gut wisdom and you feel it. Your body is your home, it is where you reside – you can't move into another body or trade it in, you can only get to know it – what makes it tick, what lights it up and makes it SHINE from the inside out. Food is a huge part of the fuel.

Owning restaurants for the past seventeen years, we have witnessed thousands of people and how they approach food. We have encountered people who have a fear of it, allergy and sensitivity issues of all kinds and how we all can restrict ourselves. We have also witnessed how food can be a celebration, healing, transformative and one of our greatest loves. What we ask is that you get real with yourself: how are you connecting with your food? how does the food you eat make you feel? Once you get a handle on the connection between how what you put into your body directly affects every single aspect of your life, we think you will understand how to EAT TO SHINE. For us it is the only way.

'YOU NEVER GET TO WHERE YOU ARE GOING WITHOUT FIRST HAVING TO EXPERIENCE THE JOURNEY, THE WRONG TURNS, THE SIDE PATHS AND THE BEAUTIFUL HORIZONS.'

We are triplet sisters, yes, born on the same day four minutes apart from each other. We have been negotiating and navigating life with each other since the womb. Life together has had its amazing highs and devastating lows, but through it all, our connection to each other has been a constant source of love and support that has weathered every storm. We grew up in a huge Italian family where food was always a centrepiece of our lives, which is a large part of what drew us into the restaurant business.

Food gives life. Food is used in times of celebration and healing; it helps bring families and friendships together. People fall in love and break up over meals. They laugh, cry and have rituals around it. Food not only feeds our bodies, but also nourishes our souls and helps us radiate from the inside out. It is directly linked to our emotional well-being. We believe the relationship you have to food is very similar to the relationship you have with yourself and how you connect to the world. As Oprah once said, '…we all gotta eat!' So we always say, why not enlighten ourselves and enjoy the ride. We ARE what we eat. The most intimate relationships we have are the ones we have with food and our bodies. Our food literally becomes us. Everything we eat influences every cell of our bodies. And so, together, we have made food our life's passion.

Together… People always ask how it came to be that we chose to stay on a similar path all these years. In a sense, it wasn't a choice, it was our destiny. As little ones, our parents chose to dress us the same and even pin name tags on each of our clothes! This has led us to constantly strive for our individuality, but here we are writing a book together. We joked that it would break us as sisters, but this process has actually brought us closer together. It has been a beautiful journey that has deepened our relationship even further.

As we got older, people were intrigued by us; three sisters who looked alike, and the way in which we connected with each other. The unconditional love between us was palpable. We come from a family where unconditional love, strength, patience and compassion were woven throughout every nook and cranny of the household. Our older brother has a rare disease called Metachromatic leukodystrophy. He is the glue of our family. He has taught us so much and has brought our family together in such a unique and fiercely loving way. He has built a bond between us that will never go away. He has been a gift in that he has taught us to stick together even in the toughest of times. He taught us to look fear and the unknown straight in the eye with love and trust. The life expectancy of his diagnosis was anywhere from three years to twenty-five years. Our brother is forty-five-years-old today and his doctors attribute his well-being over all this time directly to his care by his family. That means love and of course ensuring he gets the nutrients he needs through nutritionally dense food. He is, for us, the ultimate lesson in how important family is and that love heals.

'FOOD GIVES LIFE. FOOD IS USED IN TIMES OF CELEBRATION AND HEALING; IT HELPS BRING FAMILIES AND FRIENDSHIPS TOGETHER.'

Our mum and dad have been married for almost fifty years and have been so supportive of us and our wild roller-coaster lives over the years. We know it was no walk in the park to raise triplets on top of our brother and the extra care he needs. Growing up, our mum was a nurse on the graveyard shift in the intensive care unit in a New York City hospital and our dad was always working at least two jobs. But they never complained, they always were present for us and they did more than make it work; they thrived with us and for us and we are forever grateful. It is a gift that shines through in each and every one of our relationships.

But back to the food… At age eleven, we started working together in our uncle's grocery shop. It was there that we started to understand food, to think about where it comes from and the massive influence it has on every aspect of our existence. During our university years, we managed a restaurant together and it was a blast. We knew it was our calling to serve people in this way. Jessica and Jill went to culinary school after university while Jennifer spent time in Costa Rica teaching kids English. At the age of twenty-four, we opened our first restaurant in Boulder, Colorado and through our blood, sweat, tears and laughter, food became our offering.

The restaurant was called Trilogy and it became iconic as a restaurant and nightlife scene for live music, partying, dancing, wining and dining. It was a place where youth was explored and exploited. There were late nights and wild times, but we loved every minute of it. It was inclusive, it was about community, and it was about all walks of life communing over food, drink, music, art and dance. After nine years we were good and fried and ready to move on. So, we sold it and moved on to individual projects, family, and our lives took their own paths. And then as it always does, a shift happened…

Jennifer:

At age thirty-five, I met my partner in life Eric (Eck). I didn't know it yet though, I was still feeling it out, getting to know this frenetic, quirky young man from Connecticut. After seven months of dating, I was diagnosed with breast cancer and was in absolute shock. The night before my positive tests came back, Eck got down on one knee and asked me to marry him, regardless of the outcome. Lo! and behold, it was the kindest, most loving thing anyone has ever done for me. He was and is my silver lining. He made a commitment to go through this journey with me and my family, without even completely knowing me. We made a lifetime commitment to each other. That was six years ago. Today I am happy and healthier than I have ever been. So much of my healing has come through love and vibrant food.

Jessica:

Trilogy was quite the undertaking. I ran the kitchen for nine years and loved being in the heat of it all. I was on the line with a great crew of people. I enjoyed the fast-paced, pressure-cooker environment that a kitchen can be. After many years of this, I did however, feel the need to take it to a deeper level. I always had the desire to be a positive force in the world and I love to cook, so I wanted to join these interests and take my passion a step further.

Getting my master's degree in holistic nutrition and my certification in metabolic typing changed everything for me. The Shine menu was created with this foundation and knowledge. Not only do I put my passion for food and healing into the restaurant, I also put it into how I feed my two daughters and my husband. My knowledge in healing through food was also very important in the healing process for Jennifer. Every time I prepare a meal for another person, whether for a guest at the restaurant, family or friends, I see it as an offering of health, vibrancy and of course deliciousness!

Jill:

After the Trilogy days, I took stock. I was single, and I thought maybe I would take some time and travel. I thought maybe I would move away for a little while and find more of my autonomy, the 'who am I' without my sisters and without the restaurant. I felt like I grew up so much during those Trilogy years, but it was also so much of my identity.

Around that time Jessica and her husband became pregnant with their first child, and then Ka-BOOM!, Jennifer's diagnosis came in and everything changed. I felt lost and scared. What truly got me through was community. The way family, friends and the community rallied around my sisters and me during this time took my breath away. I learnt to be vulnerable. I learnt that always having to be strong and knowing the right answer was actually not always serving me or anyone else. I allowed myself to be held. I allowed myself to crumble and then dig deep and rebuild.

From there, all I wanted to do was serve, to help make Jennifer well and support Jessica during the amazing time of her pregnancy. This is how Shine Restaurant and Gathering Place came to be. It was a vision for an offering of not only nourishing food, but a place for all of us to congregate, celebrate, transform and heal together. It was and is such a part of me and I am honoured to do the work I do with these two kindred souls, along with our amazing Shine team. I have seen first-hand how food heals, how connection heals, and it reinforced once again how much love heals. I am forever grateful.

Back together again… Four years ago we opened Shine Restaurant and Gathering Place. It is, like this book, completely authentic and from the heart. Within the restaurant there is also an event space and our brewery where we create award-winning beers and herbal potions. This book is by family, for family, and not just brothers, sisters, parents and children, but family meaning all of us everywhere. All of our recipes have a celebratory feel because we believe in the kind of food that makes you feel good. We use pure ingredients, holistic techniques and recipes that are great for sharing. For the past seventeen-plus years, we have been feeding others through our nourishing restaurants and gatherings. Now is the time to extend our offering to you!

From the heart,

The Blissful Sisters

An Invocation...

Service will come from my heart,
this is the way of magic and power.
This is my way.

I will follow my heart and live my dreams fully.

I will listen closely.

I will share my soul's unique voice in this beautiful
symphony of life that I have been gifted.

I will show up each and every day
in my truth, in my beauty and from a place of love.

I am a creator and I get to choose how I relate with this world.

May I be a light for individuals on their path
and feel the support of others as I walk mine.

We were built for these times.

I am ready. I am willing. I am open.

Now is the time to SHINE.

Each and every day I will remember this.

From the heart...

The Blissful Sisters

THE GLORY OF GLUTEN-FREE
AND PRAISE FOR PALEO

Jennifer: *Growing up, I had a serious case of psoriasis.* Parts of my skin would get itchy and scaly, and I almost always had a sporadic rash. I would feel congested and sneezy. Eventually the straw that broke the camel's back was a full-body rash, and I knew I needed to get control of what was happening. I took a blood test and it came back positive for a gluten intolerance. I cut gluten out of my diet fifteen years ago and have never had another skin reaction. Although my sisters don't have the same sensitivity, they have chosen to eat gluten in moderation and they feel the benefits. I feel blessed to be able to own a restaurant that has a one hundred per cent gluten-free kitchen. I often feel like a kid in a sweet shop knowing I can eat anything I choose and not worry.

Gluten is a protein found in many grains such as wheat, semolina, spelt, kamut, rye and barley. It is a protein that gives bread and dough its fluffy texture and chewy nature. It's also used as a stabilising agent in many processed foods, such as salad dressings and mayonnaise. It keeps them from separating or 'breaking'. It's in everything from beauty products to packaged foods to medications and supplements.

Gluten on its own is not actually the villain. Yes, it is harder to digest than most proteins, and that in itself may be difficult for some people, but what it really comes down to is, gluten has been over processed and therefore, it has caused problems for many of us. Gluten is hidden in so many processed foods. A lot of times, it is eaten at every meal in excess. Also, wheat, barley and oats have often been sprayed with chemicals, then refined and processed until they are barely recognisable by the body and therefore hard to break down. We believe that because of this it caused many issues like sensitivities and allergies to gluten. The fact that we are eating too much of it, that it is over processed and that it is a protein that is harder to digest than most other proteins creates a perfect storm. As a result, a sensitivity started to develop in many people. If a person's digestion is compromised in any way, they will most likely have a hard time digesting gluten.

Gluten is best eaten in moderation regardless of whether you have an allergy or not. The digestion of gluten can be supported by eating it in foods that have been through a fermentation process, such as soaking glutinous grains overnight before cooking, or by eating it in sourdough breads where the fermentation process breaks down the gluten, making it easier to digest. Coeliac disease is a different story. Individuals with coeliac are not able to tolerate gluten in their diet at all and will most likely never be able to tolerate it. For them, gluten-free is a way of life.

We have chosen to create a gluten-free cookery book as well as a gluten-free restaurant because, after working in the food industry for over twenty years, we have found that many people are having issues with gluten. We have seen through our experience that going gluten-free will help heal the gut and create a stronger digestive fire, which translates into more energy and stronger health overall.

Paleo is eating close to the earth, in a way that's very similar to how our ancestors ate before the industrial age. It is, in a nutshell, eating whole unprocessed foods such as grass-fed meats, free-range chicken, wild fish, lots of fresh vegetables, natural fats and nuts and seeds, while eliminating grains and pulses and limiting dairy, unless it is raw dairy. It is cutting out foods that lead to inflammation in the body. It is said by many who have switched to this way of eating, and now even an increasing number of doctors and nutritionists, that the Paleo way of eating is energising and brings you to your body's natural and healthiest weight. It is simple, clean, easy to digest, healing and wholesome. It means eating a healthy balance of fats, proteins and carbohydrates in a culture that is inundated with processed, overly starchy and added-sugar foods.

What we like about this way of eating is that it is a framework that can be tailored to individual needs, depending on your sensitivities, genetics and desires. Our bottom line is to listen to your body and see how a variety of foods make you feel. If you know your digestion is off, your energy levels wane or you have skin irritations, it is worth switching things around, experimenting with a Paleo and gluten-free way of eating, and seeing if you experience positive changes. Your inner fire is everything. If you feel energised and inspired, life is a playground and you can engage in a playful manner.

The recipes in this book are one hundred per cent gluten-free and are Paleo-inspired. We are eighty/twenties, meaning we eat Paleo about eighty per cent of the time, so we've shared some of our favourite nutritious non-Paleo dishes with you as well.

ABOUT THE RECIPE ICONS

PI Paleo-inspired

DF Dairy-free

V Vegetarian

All recipes in the book are gluten-free

Jill: *I learnt of the Paleo way of eating* about five years ago while teaching holistic nutrition and chef instruction classes and diving into different diets that were taking hold around the country. Paleo made sense to me and intrigued me and, although I was never a dieter, this was different, it was more of a way of life and I was down to give it a whirl. I am pretty active in my day-to-day life. I try to exercise most days and am usually running around in the restaurant. I eat Paleo about eighty per cent of the time. I am not strict but I am dedicated, and by eating in this way, I feel better than I ever have in my life. I feel energised, I sleep better and I am leaner, and because of this I can participate more fully in my life.

WAKE UP & SHINE

Every morning you get to begin again. Your morning sets the tone for the rest of the day. We love fuelling up on a wholesome breakfast to feed the body, brain and spirit. These recipes are easy, fulfilling, and will get your tank, aka your glorious body, properly filled. Reset, ready and go.

'YOUR RELATIONSHIP TO FOOD AFFECTS EVERY RELATIONSHIP IN YOUR LIFE.'

BEGIN WITHIN

Get Your Game On:
Morning Routines
by the Blissful Sisters

We like to say that every day you get to begin again. Forget New Year's resolutions that are impossible to keep. Let go of the guilt and beating yourself up for something you wish you did or didn't do yesterday. Every morning your body awakens is a reset. How you start your day sets the stage. The curtain goes up and there is a motley cast of characters, whether it be your kids, your co-workers, the person driving behind you or the cashiers at your bank; they are all part of the story. Every day will be full of revelations, lessons and growth. You never know exactly where a day will take you, but you can set yourself up for success by getting in the right mindset and getting a boost of nutrition to help you feel your best.

Jill:

1. Give thanks. I wake up with gratitude for a new day and the fact that I get to choose how I want to interact with the world.

2. Drink warm water with lemon. I like to do two glasses or a one-litre Kilner jar and sometimes go as far as adding some ginger, turmeric and a little black pepper (black pepper helps with the absorption of turmeric). This not only starts my body off hydrated and kicks my metabolism into gear, but it also aids my digestion, is an anti-inflammatory, and boosts my immune system. I drink this before having any stimulants like green tea, black tea or coffee.

3. Blend a smoothie. I make a smoothie (see our smoothie recipes, starting on page 146) that includes vegetables, good fats, protein and fibre. I make sure to choose one that satiates me, so that I am not hungry an hour later, but instead feel energised until lunchtime.

4. Check in. Here's a practise that allows me to check in with how my emotional and physical body is feeling. If there is any anxiety in any part of my body, I sit, put my hands over that spot, and focus on breathing there and allowing the anxiety to release.

5. Move your body. Whether it is fifteen minutes or an hour, I leave some time to get my heart rate up most days. Then if I am sitting in front of my computer, I don't feel as much tension or body aches. (Note: If I do have to sit in front of my computer for the majority of the day, once every hour I get up and either take a walk outside for a few minutes or just take a walk around the building to get the blood flowing. I find that if I do this, I stay motivated and my brain stays in the game.)

6. Finish with coffee. I love deep rich coffee, but I try not to have it first thing and I also alternate Root to Rise Coffee (page 162) with with green tea, matcha, or maté. My caffeine intake happens after my quiet time and exercise. It helps me not get addicted to having it first thing in the morning in order to wake up.

7. Detoxify the skin. I make my own sugar scrubs, which leave my skin feeling soft and help gently release toxins from my skin. Try my recipe below. Some basic exfoliating gloves work well, too.

8. Set the mood. I turn up some of my favourite tunes. I put on clothes that make me feel good – sassy and sexy – and I head out the door, dressed the part, ready for curtain call. Bring it Life, this girl is READY.

Jennifer:

I love to wake up early enough in the morning to get some quiet time in. It is my time to get my head clear, check in with my heart and set forth on the right foot. In my daily routine, I incorporate my home-made water kefir (see recipe on page 150), a probiotic drink that keeps my digestive system healthy. I have a love affair with the stuff. I also drink warm water with lemon to aid the digestive system; it's a cleansing and detoxifying way to start the day. Most mornings I have a green juice to give me a natural energy boost instead of caffeine. I do love the flavour of coffee and tea, but I try to wake my body up through food first and have caffeine in the later part of the morning.

After my daily beverage ritual, I move my body. I love walking and hiking outside or doing yoga. It is too easy for me to hop on my computer in the morning, but I try to get in at least thirty minutes of exercise beforehand, so I can feel more energised and grounded throughout the rest of the day. I feel so blessed to live in a place where the sun shines most days. Living at a high altitude, in a sunny State, I make sure to stay well-hydrated. Making it a top priority to get movement daily helps my body and mind be in optimal health, so I can make sure I am in tiptop shape to handle all the curve balls, staff and guests that I am surrounded by at Shine every day.

Jessica:

Being the mum to two beautiful girls, aged two and five, my mornings are usually full and frenetic. My husband and I get the girls ready, make breakfast, make lunches and usually get something at least partially prepped for dinner before dropping my older girl off at kindergarten. It is important to me that the girls are well fed with nourishing foods throughout the day and that they get a good meal before they leave the house.

But back to me… After I get the girls ready, I make sure with my work schedule that I build in some time for exercise. Most often I put my younger one in a carrier on my back and hike up into the hills. This is always best done with a friend. Many times I hike with my friend who also has a baby on her back and we talk about not getting enough sleep, weaning or just finding humour in the craziness of motherhood. The support and companionship keeps me sane. I also enjoy yoga when I can get it in. If I do it at home, my girls imitate me and practise upward and downward dogs and different stretches. This is as cute as can be, but if I want to get in a deeper practise, I need to make the time and space to go to an exercise studio.

As I head in to Shine, I feel so blessed that I get to be a mum and run my own company with family. There are many times I crave more time to nurture myself, but things will shift in time and for now I am fully surrendered to motherhood and all that it brings. It is my greatest joy.

BASIC SUGAR SCRUB

I like using mostly sugar, as it is moisturising on the skin, but include some Epsom salts for extra detoxification. Make sure the granules are small so they don't scratch the skin.

Combine 180ml melted coconut oil with 60ml sesame oil for added vitamin E and its anti-ageing benefits. (You can substitute olive oil or sweet almond oil for the sesame oil, if you prefer.) The basic ratio is one part oil to two parts sugar/salt. I use 300g sugar and about 120g of Epsom salts. I also add a few drops of my favourite essential oils. Mix in a bowl with a spoon and store in a glass container. You can make it in 10 minutes; keep it in a jar in the shower and it'll turn your shower into a spa treatment!

SOFT-BOILED EGGS

Our mum is the master of the soft-boiled egg. It always felt so good to wake up to warm eggs that we could scoop right out of the shell. Just add a touch of sea salt, a dollop of ghee, and it's instant satisfaction. We love serving them with a side of cooked greens for a balanced power breakfast.

Serves 2

2 large eggs
Avocado Mash
(page 34) or
Avocado Hollandaise
(below), for serving
(optional)

1. Put the cold eggs in a small saucepan and cover them with cold water. Bring to the boil. Turn off the heat, cover the pan, and let sit for approximately 5 minutes (see Tip).

2. To eat your egg, crack the top with the back of a spoon and peel away enough shell so you can insert your spoon to scoop out the egg. Serve with Avocado Mash or Avocado Hollandaise, if you like.

TIP

The size and temperature of your eggs will have an effect on your timing. This is something to pay attention to so you can get consistent results every time.

AVOCADO HOLLANDAISE

The avocado in our 'hollandaise' sauce helps it taste rich and decadent, with a smooth consistency, even though it is egg- and dairy-free. It is easy to make and our guests at Shine go bonkers for this alternative to the classic topping for poached eggs. We also love it as a topping for greens, fish or rice, as a dipping sauce for veg and as a spread on a sandwich.

Makes about 240ml

1 ripe avocado
1 tablespoon fresh lemon juice
2 teaspoons chopped fresh dill
1 teaspoon hot sauce
120ml extra virgin olive oil
Sea salt to taste

Cut the avocado in half lengthways. Remove the stone and scoop out the avocado flesh into a food processor or high-powered blender. Process the avocado for 30 seconds or so, then add the lemon juice, dill and hot sauce and pulse two or three times. Slowly drizzle in the oil and process for a further minute until smooth and pourable. If the sauce is too thick, then add some water, a tablespoon at a time, until the desired consistency is achieved. Season with salt just before serving.

TIP

This is best made the same day you are using it for maximum flavour and freshness.

PERFECTLY POACHED EGGS WITH AVOCADO HOLLANDAISE

Served on top of our Cured Salmon and drizzled with Avocado Hollandaise, our Perfectly Poached Eggs make an Omega-3-packed power breakfast or brunch – the perfect alternative to classic Eggs Benedict. We also like them on their own, with some Avocado Mash (page 34) alongside.

Serves 2

2 medium eggs
Sea salt to taste
Avocado Hollandaise
(recipe opposite)

1. Fill a small saucepan with about 10cm of water. Bring the water to the boil and then reduce the heat to a low simmer.

2. Carefully crack each egg into a separate small bowl (careful not to break the yolks!). One at a time, very gently tip the bowls so that each egg falls into the simmering water. With a spoon, push aside any whites so they don't run into each other. Cover with a lid and turn off the heat. Your perfect poached egg will be ready in 5–7 minutes (see Tip for cooking times by preference).

3. Season with sea salt, drizzle with the avocado hollandaise, and serve immediately.

TIP
Poaching preferences:
5 minutes for soft
6 minutes for medium
7 minutes for hard poach

BAKED EGGS
IN AVOCADO CUPS

This is a power breakfast, high in protein and great fats, to make you energised as you step into your day. Smaller eggs are better to use than large ones here, as the flavour is more concentrated and they will fit better in the avocado cups. For an extra kick and added protein, serve with our Cultured Salsa (page 54) and a sprinkling of chopped crispy bacon.

Serves 2–4

2 ripe avocados
4 small free-range eggs
1 tablespoon ghee (page 30) or unsalted butter, melted
Sea salt to taste

1. Preheat the oven to 200°C/gas mark 6.

2. Cut the avocados in half lengthways and remove the stones. Using a tablespoon, scoop out 1–2 tablespoons of avocado flesh from each half to create 4 cups, each large enough to hold one of your eggs. (This is a delicate process that will result in the ideal outcome if the eggs are on the small size. Size matters here.)

3. Crack an egg into each avocado 'cup'. Yolks first followed by the whites if room allows. Drizzle each with the melted ghee and sprinkle with sea salt.

4. Arrange the avocado cups in a small baking dish to fit them as close and snug as possible. Bake for 10–12 minutes, until the egg whites look cooked through. Serve immediately.

TIP
If you have left over avocado you can rub the flesh lightly with a few drops of lemon and olive oil and cover tightly with clingfilm to keep the freshness and make the colour last longer. Best if eaten within a day or two.

Jill: Ghee is butter with the milk solids removed. It has wondrous health benefits. I add it to coffee (see our Root to Rise Coffee, page 162) and smoothies and love to cook with it. It is much more stable for high-heat cooking than regular butter and many oils because it has a higher smoke point, so it's less likely for your kitchen to get smoky. It actually has a more buttery flavour than plain butter and much more nutritional value as well. Some people who have a hard time digesting dairy can actually eat ghee. I love the smell when it is simmering on the hob. I am all about the ghee. I use it generously daily.

HOMEMADE GHEE

Makes 720ml

900g chilled unsalted butter, grass-fed when possible, cut into small cubes

1. Gather the following tools together to make your home-made ghee: a small bowl, small sieve, sterilised 1-litre glass jar, and several pieces of cheesecloth for straining the butter.

2. Melt the butter in a pan over a medium heat. When it's fully melted, let the butter come to a light simmer, then reduce the heat to low-medium (see Tip). A thick foam will start to form on the top. Continue to simmer as the foam first increases, then decreases and dissipates as the milk solids begin to attach to the sides and the bottom of the pan. Allow the solids to sink to the bottom, lightly scraping the sides of the pan with a silicone spatula to assist.

3. Continue to scrape the sides of the pan so the solids do not burn. After 5–7 minutes, the butter will start to clear as the milk solids begin to brown at the bottom of the pan. Turn off the heat once the butter begins to lightly foam again.

4. Allow the butter to cool slightly and the foam to settle, then strain the ghee through the cheesecloth into the sterilised glass jar.

5. Stored in the jar at room temperature; your ghee will keep for 2–4 months.

TIP

It is important to cook the butter over low to medium heat to help the milk solids to separate. We have found that doing this too low and too slowly sometimes creates a murky product in the end instead of the clear ghee we desire.

AMARANTH PORRIDGE

Soaking whole grains, pulses and nuts is an important step before eating these foods. They contain a coating that protects them in nature, but also makes them challenging to digest as well as making some of their nutritional value unavailable. Soaking these foods for 6 hours or overnight dissolves this coating and creates an easy to digest, highly nutritional food. We soak all grains, nuts and pulses for the restaurant. It is a challenge to do this in a high-volume restaurant, but we wouldn't have it any other way.

Serves 4–6

600ml full-fat canned coconut milk

480ml water

390g amaranth, soaked overnight and drained

2 teaspoons vanilla extract (to make your own, see page 171)

120ml maple syrup

½ teaspoon ground cinnamon

1. Pour 480ml of the coconut milk and the water into a medium pan and bring to the boil. Add the amaranth and return to the boil. Reduce the heat to a simmer and cook for 20 minutes.

2. Add the remaining 120ml coconut milk and mix well. Return the heat to medium-low and cook for a further 10 minutes, until most of the liquid is absorbed and the amaranth is tender.

3. Remove from the heat and stir in the vanilla extract and maple syrup. Sprinkle with the cinnamon (do not mix it in yet), cover the pan, and let the porridge stand for 5 minutes before serving. Refrigerate leftovers in an airtight container for up to 1 week.

TIP
This porridge is delicious served with a variety of nuts, berries, sliced banana or a dollop of ghee. It is a perfect recipe to make in advance so it's ready to just heat up in the mornings.

Jill: I went on an early morning run at our family holiday beach house and as I walked up to the house, I witnessed my mother spoon-feeding my brother this porridge. I sat and watched them. They were in silence, but there was so much love passing between them. When I went inside, my mum said to me, 'I just love taking care of him'. It was a beautiful statement about unconditional love that's emblematic of what this porridge means to me... comfort and security. My mum made farina when we were growing up and this is our family's latest hot cereal made with amaranth, an ancient gluten-free grain that is dense with minerals and has more protein than most other grains. The maple syrup in place of the white sugar we used to use adds additional minerals and just the right amount of sweetness.

SWEET POTATO AND KALE HASH

This hash can be a side dish or main, paired with eggs or Cured Salmon (page 34), or both. We like it because it is fast to make, easy to clean up (only one pan required), and a enjoyable way to get a powerful dose of vegetables. You can switch up the veg to use up whatever you have in your fridge.

Serves 4–6

2 rashers uncooked bacon (optional)

1 tablespoon coconut oil or ghee (to make your own, see page 30), plus more if needed

145g sweet potato, diced

85g assorted root vegetables, diced (we love carrots and turnips here)

55g sweet peppers, diced

30g onion, diced

1 small bunch curly kale, de-stemmed and chopped into bite-size pieces

1 teaspoon finely chopped garlic

Sea salt to taste

1. Cook the bacon, if using, in a large sauté pan over a medium-high heat, until crisp on both sides. (No oil is necessary as the bacon will render its own fat.) Remove from the pan and let cool, leaving the fat in the pan.

2. Melt the coconut oil in the pan (use only ½ tablespoon if you rendered the bacon in the pan). Add the sweet potatoes and root vegetables to the pan and sauté until mostly tender, 7–10 minutes. Add the sweet peppers and onion and cook for a further 5 minutes. Add the kale and garlic and sauté for approximately 1 minute. Season with salt and cook for a further 3–5 minutes. (If your hash becomes dry or begins to stick to the pan, add another tablespoon of coconut oil.)

3. When all the vegetables are tender and the flavours have commingled, turn off the heat and add the reserved crisp bacon, if using. Serve hot.

TIP
Add cooked minced grass-fed beef or minced turkey to make this hash a hearty one-pan meal.

CURED SALMON

It is important to use wild salmon in this recipe to get the benefit of higher Omega-3s, which support health benefits including heart health, healthy cholesterol levels and optimal brain function. Plus, wild has more flavour and a better texture. Ocean pollutants are also much more concentrated in most farmed fish. There are exceptions with sustainable farming methods, so talk to your local fishmonger to find out which seafoods are the best choices. We like to serve this with Avocado Mash (below) on toast, with eggs, or in sweet potato hash (page 33). Note: this recipe takes three days to cure, so plan accordingly!

Makes 900g

2 × 450g salmon fillets, skin on, deboned, pin bones removed
225g fine sea salt
100g granulated sugar
10 sprigs or 15g fresh dillweed
Avocado Mash
(recipe below; optional)

TIP

This mash can be made into more of a guacamole-style dip if you add 2–3 tablespoons fresh lime juice and 1 heaped tablespoon freshly chopped coriander.

1. Rinse the salmon under cold water and pat dry completely with kitchen paper. Combine the salt and sugar in a small bowl.

2. Lay out the fillets, skin sides down, on a chopping board or clean work surface. Pour the salt and sugar mixture onto the flesh, dividing it evenly between the fillets, and rub it in. Top each fillet with half of the dill sprigs.

3. Lay one piece of salmon on top of the other, with the pink fleshy parts of the fillets facing each other. Make sure you sandwich the dill in there nicely.

4. Tightly wrap the entire salmon 'sandwich' in clingfilm and put it in a shallow nonreactive container. Cover the salmon with more clingfilm. Top with something flat (a small clean chopping board is perfect) and weight the salmon down with a heavy tin.

5. Refrigerate for 3 days, flipping the salmon sandwich over every 12 hours or so. Make sure to drain and discard any accumulated liquids and reposition the weight on top of the salmon each time.

6. After 3 days, unwrap the salmon, thoroughly rinse it with water to remove all of the salt and sugar and pat it dry, keeping the two fillets sandwiched together.

7. To serve, very thinly slice the cured salmon, cutting only as much as you plan to use. Serve with avocado mash alongside, if you choose. Wrap the rest of the fillet sandwich whole in clingfilm and refrigerate on a plate or in an airtight container. The cured salmon will keep for 2–3 weeks.

AVOCADO MASH

Avocados are a superfood. They equalise blood sugar and cholesterol. Avocados are loaded with heart-healthy monounsaturated fatty acids and fibre to keep your system moving. They are a fantastic fat to incorporate into your daily diet. We serve this mash alongside our Cured Salmon (above), spread it on toast, or use it as a dip.

Makes about 360ml

2 ripe avocados
2 teaspoons finely chopped red onion
½ teaspoon finely chopped garlic
1 teaspoon apple cider vinegar
Sea salt to taste

1. Cut the avocados in half lengthways, remove the stones, and spoon out the flesh into a large bowl. Lightly mash the avocados with the back of a fork.

2. Add the red onion, garlic and vinegar to the bowl and mix together. Season with salt. Serve immediately.

RAW PALEO SPROUTED GRANOLA

This sprouted granola may sound like a lot of work, but it is worth it! Actually, most of the time that goes into this recipe is for the dehydrating process. It keeps for at least 2 months and makes a big batch so you prepare it once and enjoy it for a long time. Serve with milk or yogurt – or eat it alone as a trail mix. Just be warned: It can be addictive!

PI
DF
V

Makes 2 litre jars

140g raw shelled sunflower seeds
140g raw shelled pumpkin seeds
80g raw walnuts, chopped
100g raw almonds, chopped
120g dried cherries, chopped
140g raisins, chopped
8 dried Medjool dates, chopped
75g raw coconut flakes
120ml maple syrup
2 teaspoons vanilla extract
(to make your own, see page 171)
2 teaspoons sea salt
120ml coconut oil

1. Thoroughly wash and rinse all of the nuts and seeds. Combine in a bowl, cover with filtered water, and let soak at room temperature overnight.

2. The next morning, drain and thoroughly rinse the seeds and nuts. Spread them out on dehydrator trays and dehydrate at 40°C (or on the seed and nut setting on your dehydrator). This will take 6–8 hours, depending on your dehydrator. (If you do not own a dehydrator, see Tip.)

3. Transfer the dehydrated nuts and seeds to large bowl and toss with the dried cherries, raisins, dates and flaked coconut. Add the maple syrup, vanilla extract and salt, mixing thoroughly to coat.

4. Heat a large pan on a low heat. Add the coconut oil and let melt (this takes 1–2 minutes). Add the nut and dried fruit mixture to the coconut oil. Toss several times to coat, then remove from the heat.

5. Lay out parchment paper on two baking sheets or on the kitchen counter. Pour half of the granola mixture onto each sheet of paper, spreading it out evenly. Let harden overnight.

6. In the morning, mix the granola one more time with your hands. It will last for up to 2 months stored in a glass container in the larder.

TIP
You can also dry out the nuts and seeds at a low temperature in the oven. Arrange them on a baking sheet and place them in a very slow oven (about 45°C or the lowest your oven will go) for at least 4 hours or overnight until they are completely dried and crisp. If you are concerned about keeping the nuts raw, it is important to maintain the 45°C temperature.

GRAIN-FREE PANCAKES WITH STRAWBERRY MAPLE SAUCE

Makes 15 ×10cm pancakes;
serves 4–6

60g coconut flour
120g tapioca flour
½ teaspoon bicarbonate of soda
1 teaspoon ground cinnamon
pinch of sea salt
3 medium eggs
240ml milk of your choice
(whole milk, almond milk, or
rice milk), plus more if needed

1 teaspoon apple cider vinegar
3 tablespoons almond butter
2 tablespoons honey
1 - 2 tablespoons ghee
(to make your own, see page 30)
or coconut oil, plus more ghee
or butter for serving

Strawberry Maple Sauce
(recipe below)

1. In a small bowl, mix together both flours, bicarbonate of soda, cinnamon and salt and set aside.

2. In a large bowl, whisk the eggs. Add the milk, apple cider vinegar, almond butter and honey and stir thoroughly.

3. Add the dry ingredients to the wet ingredients and stir to combine. The batter should be thick but pourable (add more milk if needed).

4. Heat a griddle over a medium heat and then add the ghee to melt. Working in batches, ladle six scoops of batter, each about 2 tablespoons in size, onto the hot griddle. When the pancakes are bubbling on top and light-to-medium brown on the bottom, flip them over to cook on the other side. Transfer to a serving plate when done and repeat with the remaining batter.

5. Serve the pancakes with strawberry maple syrup and more ghee or butter.

TIP
If you have leftover pancakes, once they are cooled, wrap them in freezer-safe clingfilm in batches of three to five, then store them in the freezer. To reheat, separate the pancakes and pop them in a toaster, toaster oven or oven preheated to 190°C/gas mark 5.

Jessica: My kids enjoy pancakes for breakfast on occasion. For sustained energy and an even-keeled mood, I like to make sure they get a good amount of protein and fat in their breakfast. They love these pancakes, which deliver the protein and fat I require and also have the sweetness they crave.

STRAWBERRY MAPLE SAUCE

Makes about 240ml

8 - 10 strawberries, hulled
(fresh is best, but frozen
works too; see Tip)
2 teaspoons fresh lemon juice
2½ tablespoons maple syrup

Purée all of the ingredients in a high-powered blender. Heat the purée over a low heat until warm, about 5 minutes. Drizzle on top of the pancakes.

Jessica: Because my daughters love everything strawberry…

NELSON'S BUTTERMILK DROP SCONES

Our guests go crazy for these gluten-free scones, which have a cult following at the restaurant. One of our chefs, Nelson, created the recipe, which we serve with eggs or as a dipper for soups and stews, even as a decadent sandwich bread.

Makes 16 small scones

60g unsalted butter
120g tapioca flour
60g brown rice flour
60g millet flour
½ teaspoon xanthan gum
1 teaspoon sea salt
2 teaspoons baking powder
1 tablespoon chia seeds
(optional)
240ml buttermilk

1. Cut the butter into 1cm cubes and place in the freezer to chill for at least 10 minutes.

2. In a bowl, whisk together the three flours, the xanthan gum, salt, baking powder and chia seeds, if using. Transfer to a food processor. Add the cold butter and pulse 15–20 times, just until the butter-flour mixture is cut down to pea-size pieces. Chill the dough in the freezer for 15 minutes.

3. When the dough is well-chilled, add the buttermilk and mix well until it is fully incorporated and the dough is moist and slightly sticky. Roll the dough into a ball. Cover the dough with clingfilm and place in the fridge for 10 minutes.

4. Meanwhile, preheat the oven to 200°C/gas mark 6.

5. Line a baking sheet with parchment paper. Drop 8 scones, each about a tablespoon in size, onto the prepared baking sheet. Bake for about 20 minutes, until the scones are just starting to brown on top. Repeat with the remaining batter. Serve warm.

TIP
Keeping all the ingredients cold is the key to light and flaky scones.

STARTERS, BROTHS & SOUPS

These recipes can be used as healthful meal starters or as hors d'oeuvres for entertaining. Our broths are a nutritional foundation for many dishes or gratifying on their own. We are also excited to share some of our most popular, easy-to-make soups that are great to kick off a meal or serve as a main event, especially to warm your bones during the colder months. Eat. Sip. Shine.

MOVE FROM THE HEART. OPEN IT.
SHARE ITS TRUTH, ITS WISDOM, ITS POWER.
IT IS WHERE WE CREATE FROM, HEAL FROM,
GROW FROM. TAP INTO IT. IT IS INFINITE.

SWEET POTATO BUTTER

We could eat this all day long. It is a tasty substitute for ordinary butter for breads and crackers, a sandwich spread, a dipping sauce for vegetables or a garnish in soups. It is even a fantastic baby food!

Makes 1.3kg

4 large sweet potatoes (see Tip)
2 tablespoons extra virgin olive oil
½ teaspoon sea salt

1. Preheat the oven to 200°C/gas mark 6.

2. Scrub the sweet potatoes until clean and dry them with a tea towel. Gently prick each sweet potato with a fork several times.

3. Roast the sweet potatoes in a baking dish for approximately 1 hour. The sweet potatoes are done when you can easily pierce them with a fork. Let them cool for about 15 minutes.

4. Cut the sweet potatoes in half and scoop out the flesh. Put into a food processor along with the olive oil and salt. Process until creamy, about 2 minutes. Store in an airtight container in the fridge for up to 5 days.

TIP
Make sure to use sweeter potatoes for a sweeter flavour.

Jennifer: *This is my dairy-free alternative to a cheesy sauce* and has become a hit at my house parties. It's so versatile that it can go with a variety of starters, from crisps to salami. The thickness of the sauce can even hold up as a sandwich spread.

CHEEZ SAUCE

Makes about 480ml

210g raw cashew pieces
240ml filtered water
75g nutritional yeast
¼ teaspoon garlic powder
3 tablespoons fresh lemon juice
Sea salt to taste

1. Put the cashews in a bowl, cover with water, and soak for 6 hours or overnight. When the cashews are softened, rinse them thoroughly until the water runs clear.

2. Put the cashews in a food processor and process until smooth, approximately 2 minutes. Add the filtered water and continue to blend. Add the nutritional yeast, garlic powder, lemon juice and sea salt and blend until all the ingredients are incorporated and the sauce is smooth. Store in an airtight container for up to 3 days.

3. Serve over chopped fresh vegetables or radish crisps (page 46).

TIP
If you do not have time to soak the cashews and are not concerned about the recipe being raw, put the cashews in a pan, cover with water and simmer on a low to medium heat for 15–20 minutes, until soft.

RADISH CRISPS WITH ROCKET SUNFLOWER PESTO

Serves 2–4

1 large bunch radishes, greens removed
2 tablespoons extra virgin olive oil
Sea salt
Rocket Sunflower Pesto (below)

1. Preheat the oven to 180°C/gas mark 4.

2. Wash and dry the radishes thoroughly. Slice them with a mandoline or by hand. (Thinner slices will result in crunchier crisps.) Toss with olive oil and salt.

3. Arrange the radish slices in a single layer on a baking sheet. Bake for 12–15 minutes, until crisp.

4. Let cool on the baking sheet. Serve with the Rocket Sunflower Pesto as a dipping sauce (see Tip).

ROCKET SUNFLOWER PESTO

This is a fantastic dairy-free and nut-free alternative to regular pesto. The rocket adds a nice spiciness to sandwiches and pastas. We also enjoy it as a dip for our Radish Crisps (above) and even raw veg. Nutritional yeast is a deactivated yeast that contains a wide spectrum of B vitamins and trace minerals. It works great in dairy-free dishes because it adds a 'cheesy' flavour.

Makes about 480ml

2 cloves garlic, peeled
100g shelled sunflower seeds, soaked overnight then drained and rinsed
1 bunch rocket
Juice of 1 lemon
25g nutritional yeast
120ml extra virgin olive oil
Sea salt to taste

1. Put the garlic and sunflower seeds in a food processor and process for 2 minutes. Add the rocket and lemon juice and process for 1 minute. Add the nutritional yeast and pulse until fully incorporated.

2. Slowly drizzle in the olive oil while processing until the pesto is smooth. Season with sea salt.

3. Serve immediately or store in a glass container. The pesto will keep in the fridge, covered tightly, for up to 5 days.

TIP

When the recipe is finished, check the consistency. If you are looking for a thinner sauce, add 1 tablespoon of water at a time until you achieve your desired consistency.

WHY IS FERMENTATION ALL THE RAGE?

Fermentation, which can also be called culturing, is an age-old, tried-and-true method of preparing food that will help keep your body in optimal health. Some fermented foods that we eat and drink regularly are certain breads, chocolate, cheese, certain teas, pickles, yogurt, to name a few as well as wine, beer and spirits (in moderation). The main reason we eat fermented food is to support digestion and promote a healthy gut, because this is the foundation of assimilation. Assimilation is how your body processes all of the nutrients that turn your food into fuel and that affects everything. Without good digestion, it doesn't matter what you eat, the cells just don't receive it.

Fermenting will help you assimilate your food. It's as simple as that, yet, we believe it is the key that unlocks the door to optimal health within your body and your life. Sandor Katz, who wrote the amazing book *The Art of Fermentation*, says 'the creative space between fresh and rotten is the root of most of humanity's prized delicacies'. It's true! Fermented food uses time and temperature to help good bacteria proliferate in food, which not only helps preserve the food and deepen the flavours, but also helps heal our guts and keep our bodies balanced and healthy.

A simple way to think of it is that fermented foods are partially digested, which makes it very easy for our bodies to break them down and absorb their nutrients. Fermentation not only aids digestion; it boosts the immune system, enhances the nutrient content of food and increases your body's energy to name a few of the benefits. And fermenting foods is surprisingly easy! In these days of processed foods and mass production, we have lost this ancient tradition and our bodies have suffered for it. Well, now is the time to bring it back! Your belly is about to get really happy…

Raw cultured vegetables are powerful superfoods. We've included quick and easy recipes for Cultured Salsa (page 54) and Cultured Carrots and Ginger (page 52). Adding just a few tablespoonfuls a day of these veg to your diet will give you amazing health benefits, such as reducing the pH levels in your body to create a more alkaline environment. (Diseases thrive in acidic environments.) Always use clean organic vegetables for cultured recipes. If there are any pesticides or other chemicals in the vegetables, the toxins will become more concentrated during fermentation.

Soaking or sprouting your nuts, seeds, grains and pulses is another form of fermentation; many examples of this are in the book. These techniques help release digestive enzymes, making even hard-to-digest foods much easier on our digestive systems so we can actually soak up all the nutrients these miracle foods have to offer. In fact, soaking and sprouting not only helps our bodies absorb vitamins, they actually increase the vitamin levels. Below are basic recipes for soaking nuts and sprouting seeds; no dehydrator or sprouting machine needed. If you choose, you can use soaked or sprouted ingredients even in recipes that don't specifically call for them.

A BASIC RECIPE FOR SOAKING NUTS

Makes about 400g

400g raw nuts, such as walnuts, almonds or cashews
1 tablespoon sea salt
2-litre Kilner jar
1 litre filtered water

1. Combine the nuts and salt in a 2-litre glass jar and add the filtered water. Let the nuts soak for at least 7 hours or overnight.

3. Drain and rinse and lay out on a sheet pan.

2. Place the pan in a very slow oven (about 65°C, or the lowest temperature your oven will go). Let the nuts dry for approximately 7 hours, or until completely dry.

3. Store in the fridge in an airtight container. They will last about 1 month, depending on the type of nut.

A BASIC RECIPE FOR SPROUTING SEEDS

Makes about 75g sprouts

40g raw organic sprouting seeds, such as fenugreek, radish or quinoa (see Tip)
2-litre Kilner jar with sprouting lid
Filtered water

1. Put the seeds in a Kilner jar and fill with enough water to cover the seeds. Put the sprouting lid on top, swirl the jar to rinse the seeds and pour the water off while straining it through the lid.

2. Add more water using enough to cover the seeds by 10cm and put the sprouting lid back on. Soak for at least 6 hours or overnight.

3. Rinse the seeds and drain well.

4. Let the seeds sit in the Kilner jar without water at room temperature for 24–72 hours to let them sprout. During this time, rinse them every 6–8 hours. The sprouts are ready when you see a little tail that is approximately the same length as the original seed.

5. Rinse the sprouts thoroughly and store in the fridge for up to 5 days.

TIP
You need to use raw, whole, organic seeds for the sprouting process to be successful.

CULTURED CARROTS AND GINGER

This is a sweet and tart garnish for seafood, salad, or soups. Just a tablespoon will aid in digestion. Culturing heightens the levels of nutrients that are already present in food, as well as adding enzymes and probiotics for gut health. See 'Why Is Fermentation All the Rage?' on page 48 for more reasons why we are big fans of culturing.

Makes one about 1kg

720ml filtered water

3 tablespoons sea salt

1kg fresh carrots, trimmed and cut into matchsticks or shredded

2 tablespoons peeled and finely chopped fresh ginger

2-litre Kilner jar

1 large outer cabbage leaf

1. To make the brine, bring 240ml of the filtered water to the boil. Add the salt, stirring to dissolve. Once the salt is completely dissolved, add the remaining 480ml of room temperature filtered water. Remove from the heat and let cool.

2. Combine the carrots and ginger in a sterilised 2-litre Kilner jar. Once the brine has cooled to room temperature, pour it over the carrot mixture, pushing the carrots down so that they are completely submerged in the brine.

3. Tightly and entirely cover the carrot and ginger mixture with the large cabbage leaf. This will help keep the fermentation process free of oxygen, which can cause mould. Leave 2.5cm headspace and screw on the lid.

4. Put the jar in a cool room or cupboard (18°C to 22°C is ideal). Allow the carrots to culture (ferment) for 7–10 days (see Tip), or as long as desired.

5. Refrigerate the jar after opening. The cultured carrots will last for up to 3 months in the fridge.

TIP

Make sure to 'burp' your jar every day for the first 3 or 4 days of the fermentation process to let the gas escape. Do this by unscrewing the cap, removing it for a couple of seconds, and then screwing on the cap securely again. Sterilise your jar either in your dishwasher or by boiling the jars in a large pan.

CULTURED SALSA

Everyone loves crisps and salsa, and we have mastered a way to up the ante on digestion and the health benefits of the tomatoes through fermentation. The longer this salsa cultures, the more flavour it has. Serve it with tacos, crisps or Bean-free Chilli (page 114), Avocado Mash (page 34), Baked Eggs in Avocado Cups (page 28), or fish dishes.

PI
DF
V

Makes about 1.4 litres

1.3kg ripe plum tomatoes, cut into medium dice

1 small onion, diced

2 tablespoons chopped coriander

2½ tablespoons sliced spring onions

1½ tablespoons finely chopped garlic

1 tablespoon seeded and finely chopped jalapeño pepper

1 teaspoon ground cumin, toasted briefly in a frying pan just until fragrant

4 tablespoons fresh lime juice

1 tablespoon sea salt

2-litre Kilner jar

Put all the ingredients in a large bowl and stir to combine. Pour into a clean 2-litre Kilner jar and screw on the lid. Put the jar in a cool spot, ideally between 18°C and 22°C for 2–3 days, depending on your preference in flavour. As it sits longer, the flavour becomes brighter and more effervescent. After culturing, store in a glass container and refrigerate for up to 10 days.

TIP

Topping with a cabbage leaf as in the Cultured Carrots and Ginger is not necessary for this ferment. The acid in the tomatoes and lime help protect from mould, and the shorter fermentation time also reduces the possibility of mould. You can also skip the fermentation process for a simple delicious salsa that you can eat right away!

BEETROOT HOUMOUS

Makes about 600ml

4 medium whole beetroots, peel on, scrubbed to remove any dirt

2 tablespoons extra virgin olive oil

Sea salt to taste

4 tablespoons tahini (sesame seed paste)

4 tablespoons fresh lemon juice

1 - 2 cloves garlic, roughly chopped (see Tip)

1. Preheat the oven to 190°C/gas mark 5.

2. Rub the beetroots with olive oil and a touch of salt. Put them on a baking sheet and roast for approximately 1 hour, until the beetroots are easily pierced through with a fork. Let cool slightly.

3. When the beetroots are cool enough to handle, rub the skins off with a clean dishcloth (be forewarned – the beetroots will stain it) or use a vegetable peeler. Coarsely chop the beetroots and put in them in a food processor with the remaining ingredients. Blend until smooth.

4. Serve with your favourite chopped veg or flatbread. Refrigerate leftovers, if any, in an airtight container for up to 5 days.

TIP
Since the garlic is raw, it will add a pungent garlic flavour to the houmous. You can use just 1 clove, if you prefer, or roast the garlic for a softer flavour.

Jennifer: *Beetroots have always been a favourite of mine.* I love their deep colour. This houmous is eye candy on the table at Shine, where it is one of our most popular shared starters. It has no beans – just the beauty of the beetroot, sesame paste, garlic and lemon.

RAW SPROUTED QUINOA TABBOULEH

Because this tabbouleh is completely raw, yet sprouted, it is a highly digestible and power-packed superfood! Sprouted seeds are rich in enzymes, which are healing for the body and also help digest everything you eat with them. Quinoa is technically a seed, which makes it higher in protein than grains. We serve this recipe at our restaurant with our beetroot houmous; it is also great on sandwiches, salads, and fish. The herbs and crunch from the radishes, cucumber, and tomatoes add a vibrant texture to the tabbouleh.

DF
V

Makes about 1kg

170g quinoa, soaked overnight in water until sprouted (about 12 hours; see Tip)

50g radishes, diced

40g cucumber, diced

4 cherry tomatoes, diced

15g spring onions, cut on the diagonal into small pieces

10g chopped fresh parsley

6g chopped fresh mint leaves

1 clove garlic, finely chopped

4 tablespoons fresh lemon juice

120ml extra virgin olive oil

Sea salt to taste

1. Drain and rinse the quinoa then put it in a mixing bowl. Add the radishes, cucumber, tomatoes, spring onions, parsley and mint and toss to combine.

2. In a small bowl, whisk together the garlic, lemon juice and olive oil. Pour the dressing over the quinoa mixture and toss to coat. Season with salt.

3. Leftovers may be stored in the fridge for up to 4 days.

TIP
Because of the temperature of your kitchen possibly being too cool sometimes, the quinoa may not sprout in the 12 hours specified in the recipe. If you do not see a small sprout coming from the seed, drain and rinse the quinoa anyway, but put the seeds back in your soaking container without water and let them sit in the container for a further 6–8 hours or overnight. They should be sprouted by then. Rinse and continue with the recipe.

KALE CRISPS

These kale crisps are crunchy, tender, savoury and addictive – an easy way to get kids and adults eating one of the most nutrient-dense foods on the planet. They are great with sandwiches as an alternative to potato crisps. They also do well as a side to steak, chicken or fish.

Serves 2–4

1 bunch curly kale
1 tablespoon coconut oil
½ tablespoon gluten-free tamari
1 ½ tablespoons nutritional yeast

1. Preheat the oven to 190°C/gas mark 5.

2. Wash the kale leaves and dry them well. (You can use a salad spinner and then blot the leaves dry on a kitchen towel.) To de-stem the kale, hold a piece of kale by the stem in one hand, then starting at the stem end, run your other hand along the length of the stem, ripping off the leaves as you go (see Tip). Repeat with the rest of the kale. Cut or tear the leaves into bite-size pieces and put them in a bowl.

3. Add the coconut oil and tamari to the kale and massage for 2 minutes, until the kale is soft and slightly darker.

4. Spread the kale out on two ungreased baking sheets, put both in the oven, and set the timer for 4 minutes. Pull the kale out of the oven and sprinkle with the nutritional yeast, give it a quick mix, and put it back in the oven for a further 4 minutes until crisp.

5. Transfer the kale crisps to a serving plate and serve immediately. Or let them cool thoroughly, then store them in a tightly covered Kilner jar or glass container. They'll stay crisp for up to 3 days.

TIP

The kale stems can be saved and used in smoothies or in Pressed Green Juice (page 157). For an Italian-style version, flavour the kale leaves with garlic salt, Romano cheese (if you eat dairy) and lemon juice before baking.

The Beef on Broths:
Bone and Vegetable Broths

Bone broth and vegetable broth are amazing elixirs that provide vitamins and minerals that are easily absorbed into our bodies. The inner part of the bones contains astounding health benefits, and slow-cooking them in water releases all of their goodness into the broth. Vegetables that are cooked in this way also release a rich nutritional content and they are very alkalising, which helps keeps your body in a healthy balance. Broths can be used as a base for soups and sauces or sipped throughout the day like a tea. Vegetable broth can be seasoned with sea salt before sipping.

Bone broths are high in gelatine, which is beneficial to our hair, skin, nails, joints, connective tissue and also our guts. They help heal our intestines and are especially beneficial to those dealing with leaky gut and other digestive ailments. They are high in trace minerals that may be hard to get from other sources. For those people who don't eat dairy, they provide a solid dose of calcium. When regularly drinking vegetable and bone broths, you will notice clearer skin, your digestion will be on track and it will absolutely help with inflammation or pain in the body. It also helps curb hunger. They are amazing for an all-round healthy immune system and are deeply healing for the body.

You can start with either raw bones or cooked (meaning that if you roast a whole chicken, you can repurpose the bones to make a broth). For vegetables, start with organic raw vegetables. Using bones from organic grass-fed cattle, sheep and free-range chickens and using organic vegetables is important here. You are slow-cooking to pull out all of the components of the ingredients, so you want to make sure they are clean and pure with no added chemicals, hormones or antibiotics. Using apple cider vinegar during the cooking process of bone broth helps to draw the minerals out of the bones to get the optimal amount of nutrients from them.

Broths and stocks are some of the most nourishing foods you can put in your body. They hydrate, heal and load you up with tons and tons of minerals, warding off colds and sickness. For optimal health and all-round wellness, why not make broth a part of your everyday routine? Your body will thank you!

Jessica: During the cooler months, I have broths going all the time either on my stovetop or in my slow cooker. This is my savior during the cold season, especially having two young kids, both to build up the immune system, as well as for healing from a cold. My kids drink a little bit each morning with breakfast. They still may get runny noses, but it helps speed up healing time and gives them and me protection. I make sure the broth is strained well and add a touch of sea salt.

VEGETABLE BROTH

Vegetable broth can be seasoned with sea salt and sipped throughout the day or used as a base for soups and sauces. We like the addition of seaweed to add to the mineral content and flavour of this broth.

Makes about 2 litres

1 small onion, chopped

2 medium carrots, chopped

3 sticks celery, chopped

2 large cloves garlic, crushed

½ bunch curly kale or Swiss chard (chard will turn your broth a light purple)

45g mushroom stems

1 handful fresh flat-leaf parsley leaves

1 large piece seaweed, preferably dulse or wakame, (optional)

about 2.4 litres filtered water, or more if needed to cover ingredients

1. Combine all of the ingredients in a large stockpot, ensuring there is enough water to cover the vegetables completely, and bring to the boil. Reduce the heat and simmer for 1 hour 30 minutes to 2 hours (see Tip). Remove from the heat and let cool for about 20 minutes so it is easier to handle.

2. Strain the broth through a fine-mesh sieve into one or several airtight containers. Refrigerate for up to 5 days, or freeze for future use.

TIP

We like using tempered Kilner jars to store broth. They can handle the heat. If you are freezing the broth, leave at least 8cm at the top of the jar to allow room for expansion. Vegetable broths are simmered for a shorter amount of time than bone broth because they can get bitter if cooked too long. Also, when cooking bones, you need a longer amount of cooking time to draw out the minerals and flavour. This happens much more quickly with vegetable broth.

BEEF BONE BROTH

We always use organic bones from grass-fed animals when we make our beef bone broth. Beef broth is richer, darker, and meatier than chicken broth, so keep that in mind as you use it in soups and other recipes.

Makes about 2 litres

1 tablespoon extra virgin olive oil

900g grass-fed beef bones with marrow

180g tomato purée (see Tip)

2 tablespoons raw apple cider vinegar

About 2.4 litres filtered water, or more if needed to cover ingredients

1 medium onion, coarsely chopped

2 small carrots, peeled and coarsely chopped

2 sticks celery, coarsely chopped

5 sprigs parsley

5 sprigs thyme

1 bay leaf

1. Preheat the oven to 200°C/gas mark 6.

2. Lightly grease a baking sheet with the olive oil. Spread the bones out on the sheet and brush them liberally with the tomato purée. Roast the bones for about 25 minutes, turning them once so they brown on all sides.

3. In a large stockpot, combine the roasted bones, vinegar and filtered water, ensuring there is enough water to cover the bones. Bring to the boil. Reduce the heat and simmer for 4–6 hours, occasionally skimming off any foam that comes to the top and adding more water if needed to keep bones covered.

4. Add the onion, carrots, celery, parsley, thyme and bay leaf and continue to cook for a further 2 hours. Remove from the heat and let cool for about 20 minutes for easier handling.

5. Strain the broth through a fine-mesh sieve into one or several airtight containers and put them in the fridge to chill.

6. Skim off the fat that congeals on the top as it chills. Refrigerate the broth for up to 5 days, or freeze for future use.

TIP
If you have a sensitivity to nightshades, you may leave the tomato purée out, as it is mainly included to add sweetness to the broth.

CHICKEN BONE BROTH

Ask your butcher for high-quality organic and free-range chicken bones (or you can even use the bones from roasted chicken). Broths are great to keep your immune system strong and to help heal a common cold and body inflammation. We enjoy this chicken broth as a sipping tea or as a base for sauces or soups. See 'The Beef on Broth' (page 60) for more information about the uses and powerful benefits of broth.

Makes about 2 litres

900g bony chicken parts
(bone-in necks, backs, wings and feet)

Gizzards of 1 chicken (optional)

2 tablespoons raw apple cider vinegar

About 2.4 litres filtered water, or more if needed to cover ingredients

1 medium onion, coarsely chopped

2 small carrots, peeled and coarsely chopped

2 sticks celery, coarsely chopped

5 sprigs parsley

5 sprigs thyme

1 bay leaf

1. In a large stockpot, combine the bones, gizzards, if using, vinegar and filtered water, ensuring there is enough water to cover the bones. Bring to the boil. Reduce the heat and simmer for 4–6 hours (see Tip), occasionally skimming off any foam that comes to the surface and adding more water if needed to keep bones covered.

2. Add the onion, carrots, celery, parsley, thyme and bay leaf and continue to simmer for a further 2 hours. Remove from the heat and let cool for about 20 minutes so that it is easier to handle.

3. Strain the broth through a fine-mesh sieve into one or several airtight containers and put them in the fridge to chill.

4. Skim off the fat that congeals on the top as it cools. Refrigerate the broth for up to 5 days, or freeze for future use.

TIP
The longer you cook the chicken bones, the richer and more flavourful the broth will be. However, it is best to cook the vegetables for a maximum of 2 hours.

SQUASH AND PEAR SOUP WITH SPICED COCONUT MILK

This is an autumn soup that nourishes the lungs and warms the body. It is the perfect soup to serve at the start of the cooler weather, when we are more susceptible to colds. This soup hits the right balance between spiced and sweet that is pleasing to every generation. Plus, it just feels good going down.

Serves 6–8

1.3kg acorn or butternut squash

2 tablespoons coconut oil, plus more for brushing

30g yellow onion, chopped

1 stick celery, chopped

2 pears, peeled, cored and chopped

Sea salt to taste

1 litre vegetable or chicken stock (to make your own, see page 62 or 64)

120ml full-fat canned coconut milk

4 tablespoons maple syrup

1 teaspoon peeled and finely chopped fresh ginger

1 teaspoon ground cinnamon

1 pinch ground nutmeg

2 teaspoons vanilla extract (to make your own, see page 171)

3 tablespoons chopped raw pecans

1. Preheat the oven to 180°C/gas mark 4.

2. Cut the squash in half lengthways and scoop out the seeds. Brush the fleshy sides with coconut oil and place, flesh-side down, on a baking sheet. Bake until tender, 35–40 minutes.

3. Meanwhile, heat the coconut oil in a stockpot and sauté the onion, celery and pear with a bit of salt until softened and lightly caramelised.

4. Add the stock to the pan and simmer for 30 minutes, uncovered.

5. Scoop the roasted squash out of the peel and add to the simmering stock. Stir in the coconut milk, maple syrup, ginger, cinnamon, nutmeg and vanilla extract and simmer for a further 30 minutes.

6. Purée the soup with a high-powered hand blender or in batches in a high-powered blender until smooth. Start blending slowly first before running at a higher speed to avoid splashing hot soup.

7. Serve in bowls garnished with the pecans.

TIP

For a hearty main dish, add some protein to this soup by including a scoop of pulled chicken or beef in the centre of each bowl.

VEGAN WILD MUSHROOM BISQUE

(PI DF · V)

Serves 6–8

1 small head cauliflower, florets separated and chopped

5 tablespoons extra virgin olive oil

Sea salt to taste

210g raw cashew pieces, rinsed (see Tip)

1 large apple, chopped

200g assorted fresh mushrooms, chopped

1 shallot, finely chopped

120ml dry white wine

1 teaspoon fresh thyme leaves

2 teaspoons finely chopped fresh sage

1.4 litres vegetable stock (to make your own, see page 62)

1 pinch ground nutmeg

1. Preheat the oven to 190°C/gas mark 5.

2. In a mixing bowl, toss the cauliflower with 3 tablespoons of the olive oil and season with salt. Pour onto a baking sheet and roast until tender and lightly browned, approximately 20 minutes.

3. Rinse the cashews, place in a small pan and add enough water to cover. Bring the cashews to the boil, then reduce the heat and simmer for 30 minutes.

4. Meanwhile, heat the remaining 2 tablespoons olive oil in a wide-based pan. Add the apples and mushrooms with a dash of salt and sauté until soft and caramelised. Add the shallot and sauté for a further 5 minutes. Pour the wine into the pan and simmer until the liquid is reduced by two-thirds.

5. Stir in the roasted cauliflower, thyme and sage. Add the vegetable stock (see Tip) and bring to the boil. Reduce the heat and simmer for 30 minutes.

6. Meanwhile, drain and rinse the cooked cashews. Put the cashews in a high-powered blender and add just enough water to cover them. Blend on high speed until the cashew mixture is silky smooth and creamy. Pulse in the nutmeg.

7. Working in batches, purée the soup with the cashew cream in a blender or with a hand blender until smooth. Return the soup to the pan and simmer for a further 10 minutes to develop the flavours.

TIP

We like to rinse nuts and seeds before using them to remove any debris or residue. You can play with the consistency of the bisque by adding or reducing the amount of vegetable stock you add.

ALL DRESSED UP

We have an ongoing love affair with creative salads. This is where seasonality and local ingredients get really fun. Eating with the seasons is something we are very passionate about. As a matter of fact, we have built our restaurants around this concept. Eating what is in season is the most nutritious way of eating because eating seasonally typically leads to eating locally. And when you can buy food more locally, not only does it have more nutritional value, but it also tastes better. There is nothing like eating an apple that has been picked fresh off a tree rather than one that has been flown across the world. Eating locally also supports your local economy and helps connects you to your food and where it is coming from.

Why We Dig on Whole Foods

When the three of us went off to university, it was at the height of the low-fat, low-carb craze that seemed to have swept the nation. The truth of the matter is, each of us was at the heaviest weight we have ever been. In our fridges and cupboards, there was everything from low-fat soured cream and fat-free crisps to low-fat cheeses – if it came in low fat, we were on it. Hip-hip-hooray, a shortcut to keeping all things 'light'! The more we indulged, the more the pounds packed on. It took some time to come to grips with it, to put down the 'lite' beer and the bag of fat-free potato crisps and ask, 'Ok, what gives?' This was a shortcut that was not working.

Right around that time, we took a family trip along Highway 1 through California. Individually we were each having an eye-opening experience: Looking at all the farms as we passed by and taking in the artichokes and cabbages, herds of cows and stands with tons of veg, meats, raw milk and yogurts, we thought how vibrant and beautiful the food looked and how ALIVE. It got us talking about organic foods, local foods and whole foods. It got us thinking about the effect of what we put in our mouths and bodies. The food at these farms was beautiful and tasted amazing, like nothing we had ever experienced before. It was alive and nourishing. We were so happy to give our money to the farmers that actually grew it. We were supporting something we could believe in. It all started to make sense.

That was it, we were hooked. There was no turning back. We knew as we furthered our career in food, that it was about nourishing people from the inside out, it was about supporting the local economy and eating foods close to the earth. We made the conscious choice to make this one of the foundations of our restaurant. Jessica got her Masters degree in holistic nutrition to get a better understanding of the science of the whole foods approach and healing through foods. Holistic means 'whole body' and it influenced how we created menus and every aspect of the restaurants we ran, events we hosted, and how we lived our day-to-day lives.

Gone were the cupboards of salty snacks and cereals loaded with ingredients we didn't know how to pronounce, gone were the dairy products that contained additives and preservatives and chemicals to strip the molecules from nourishing fat cells. Our shelves became stocked with wholesome fats (see 'Fat Is Fabulous', page 164) and farm-fresh milk and yogurt that retained all the delicious taste and live digestive enzymes that help keep the gut healthy. We began eating local meats and vibrant vegetables grown either in our gardens or by local farmers.

We felt so satiated and energised and the pounds just melted off. We came back to our healthy natural weights in no time. We felt fabulous knowing we weren't ingesting pesticides and hormones when we chose organic whole foods and we weren't going to feed them to our guests or families either. We learnt that whole foods are way more potent, hold a higher nutritional value, contain more antioxidants and keep the immune system strong. Today we start with whole foods for all of our recipes and prepare them in ways that hold on to the nutritional benefits and in some cases actually increase the nutritional content (see 'Why Is Fermentation All the Rage?' on page 48).

Food is the ultimate medicine; it can heal, prevent disease, energise your body. Eating whole foods without pesticides and hormones. is a commitment to yourself and to the health of the planet. It's saying YES, you want to live a life of optimal health. For us, it is now the only way – we are forever grateful to the farmers.

Here are some fun ideas to help you stay connected with your vegetables:

- Contact the Soil Association to find an organic veg box scheme: a great way to get fresh, healthy organic fruit and vegetables delivered straight to your door or to a local collection point. You pay a weekly subscription for which you get an array of seasonal fruits and vegetables. It encourages creativity because you never know exactly what you are going to get! Some schemes offer dairy, meat and fish as well.

- Grow your own! Even with just a small plot of soil, you can grow a good amount of vegetables. Kale is easy to grow, as are many greens and herbs. Pick some of your favourite vegetables and go for it! Gardening is fun, educational and wildly nutritious for the whole family.

CAESAR SALAD WITH ROASTED CHICKPEAS

Our version of Classic Caesar dressing has been a staple for years. We love it as a dip for cold chicken, with raw veg, on sandwiches and, of course, as a salad dressing. We like to make it in bigger batches and stash it in the fridge so it's at the ready for snacking.

The vegan version is a favourite at Shine restaurant. It is unique in the way that the dulse seaweed takes the place of the anchovy and the almonds create the silky texture traditionally provided by the eggs. Dulse has a salty, oceany flavour and helps cleanse the body of heavy metals and supports brain function and healthy thyroid function.

Serves 4–6

FOR THE CLASSIC CAESAR DRESSING (OR USE VEGAN CAESAR DRESSING, PAGE 77):

2 medium soft-boiled eggs (page 26; see Tip)

4 tablespoons fresh lemon juice

3 cloves garlic, finely chopped

¾ tablespoon anchovy paste (see Tip)

1 teaspoon Worcestershire sauce (check label to make sure it is gluten-free)

½ teaspoon Dijon mustard

40g Pecorino Romano cheese, shredded

240ml extra virgin olive oil

FOR THE SALAD

3 heads cos lettuce hearts, torn into bite-size pieces

35g Roasted Chickpeas (page 76)

1. First make the dressing: put all of the ingredients in a food processor except the olive oil and blend for 30–60 seconds. With the food processor running, slowly drizzle the olive oil down the chute to emulsify the dressing into a creamy consistency.

2. Put the cos lettuce and roasted chickpeas in a salad bowl. Add the dressing and toss to coat.

TIP

Feel free to get creative with your Caesar. We sometimes add crumbled bacon, soft-boiled egg, roasted tomatoes or all three!

We like to soft-boil the eggs used in this dressing in order to make people feel comfortable with its safety and for their taste, but this dressing can also be made with raw pasteurised eggs. Anchovy is a strong flavour. You may want to start with less, then taste before your final mixing to see if you want add the full amount.

ROASTED CHICKPEAS

Chickpeas, also known as garbanzo beans in the US, are an Italian staple. Rich in fibre, they aid in digestion and help stabilise blood sugar. We added them to every salad while we were growing up. This is a more sophisticated version of that salad topper and an alternative to croutons that also adds crunch and flavour.

Makes about 240g

240g cooked chickpeas (if using canned, choose a 400g tin)
2 tablespoons extra virgin olive oil
½ teaspoon sea salt
1 teaspoon garlic powder

1. Preheat the oven to 200°C/gas mark 6.

2. Rinse and drain the chickpeas in a sieve, place them on a clean tea towel and pat them a few times to dry.

3. Whisk the olive oil, salt and garlic powder together in a mixing bowl. Add the chickpeas and toss to coat. Spread them out evenly on a baking sheet.

4. Roast the chickpeas for 20 minutes. Gently shake the baking sheet to move them around, and then bake them for a further 5 minutes until lightly golden.

5. Serve straight out of the oven. The chickpeas will keep for up to 4 days at room temperature in a sealed container.

TIP

There are many different things you can do with the flavouring of these chickpeas. Some of our favourites are shaking on curry powder or an Italian herb blend, or tossing the chickpeas in melted ghee and Pecorino Romano cheese.

Jessica: My daughter Amelie loves munching on these chickpea snacks while she is on my back on the hiking trail.

VEGAN CAESAR DRESSING

Makes about 600ml

130g blanched (skinless) almonds (see Tip), soaked for 3 hours or simmered for 20 minutes

300ml filtered water

2 cloves garlic, peeled

180ml fresh lemon juice

1 tablespoon plus 1 teaspoon dulse flakes

25g nutritional yeast

2 teaspoons Dijon mustard

1 tablespoon capers plus 2 teaspoons of the brine

1 teaspoon sea salt

180ml extra virgin olive oil

Put all of the ingredients except for the oil in a blender and run it for 1 minute. With the blender running, slowly drizzle in the olive oil for a creamy finish.

TIP

Blanched almonds work best in this recipe. If you can't find them in the shop, blanching natural almonds to remove their skins is an easy process. Begin by bringing a small pan of water to the boil. Place the almonds in the water for exactly 1 minute. If you boil them any longer, the almonds will become too soft. Drain the almonds in a colander and rinse under cold water to cool them. Blot them with kitchen paper and use your fingers to gently squeeze the almonds to loosen and remove the skins.

ROCKET, PEAR AND BLUE CHEESE SALAD WITH HONEY WALNUT VINAIGRETTE

When using blue cheeses, note that not all of them are gluten-free. If this concerns you, check the packaging to be sure. The walnuts in the dressing add flavour, texture and a protein boost.

Serves 4–6

FOR THE HONEY WALNUT VINAIGRETTE

50g walnut pieces

2 tablespoons finely chopped shallots

4 tablespoons red wine vinegar

1 tablespoon raw honey

½ teaspoon dried thyme (optional)

240ml extra virgin olive oil

4 tablespoons filtered water

Sea salt to taste

FOR THE SALAD

40g baby rocket

55g blue cheese, crumbled

170g peeled, cored and diced pear

35g dates, chopped

1. First make the dressing: put all of the ingredients in the blender except for the olive oil and water and blend thoroughly. While still blending, slowly add the olive oil. Add the water slowly to get the desired consistency. You may not need all of it. Salt to taste.

2. Put all of the ingredients in a salad bowl and toss with the Honey Walnut Vinaigrette to coat.

TIP

In winter it could be hard to find rocket but you can swap it with another green such as spinach or mixed salad leaves.

KALE AND HIJIKI SALAD WITH ORANGE TAHINI DRESSING

Hijiki is a type of seaweed. Some of its greatest health benefits are balancing hormonal activity, improved energy levels, and strengthening for bones. This salad is a powerhouse of nutrition and delivers in flavour. Pan-seared Fish (page 92) or Pan-Seared Bone-In Chicken Thighs (page 94) is a great addition to this salad.

Serves 3–4

FOR THE ORANGE TAHINI DRESSING
240ml orange juice
75g raw tahini (sesame seed paste)
120ml extra virgin olive oil
4 tablespoons avocado oil
1 teaspoon apple cider vinegar
1 teaspoon gluten-free tamari
Sea salt to taste

FOR THE SALAD
4 tablespoons dried hijiki seaweed
50g shiitake mushrooms, sliced and stems removed
1 tablespoon extra virgin olive oil
1½ teaspoons gluten-free tamari
80g curly kale leaves, chopped
135g carrots, grated
½ cucumber, peeled and julienned
2 tablespoons sesame seeds, to garnish (optional)

1. First make the dressing: combine all of the ingredients in a blender and blend for 1 minute until creamy.

2. Rinse the hijiki, cover with water, and soak for 20–30 minutes until tender. Drain, rinse, and set aside.

3. Meanwhile, in a mixing bowl, toss the shiitake mushrooms with the olive oil and tamari. Marinate for 15 minutes.

4. To the bowl of marinated mushrooms, add the kale, carrots, cucumbers, and sesame seeds, along with the drained hijiki. Drizzle the salad with the dressing and toss to coat. Serve immediately.

TIP
Tahini can be expensive. You can easily make your own by blending 125g sesame seeds with 2 tablespoons mild olive oil or sesame oil. This homemade tahini can be stored for up to 1 month in the fridge.

CHOPPED GARDEN SALAD WITH DAIRY-FREE RANCH

PI
DF

Ranch is one of the most popular – and least healthy – dressings out there. Our dairy-free version is a fantastic alternative that makes a wonderful salad dressing, dip for crisps and vegetables, as well as a sauce for fish sticks (page 100) and chicken fingers (page 105).

Serves 4–6

FOR THE DAIRY-FREE
RANCH DRESSING:

115g mayonnaise, shop-bought
or home-made (page 98)

120ml full-fat canned coconut milk

1 teaspoon raw apple cider vinegar

2 teaspoons chopped fresh dillweed

1 tablespoon chopped fresh chives

1 teaspoon chopped fresh parsley

½ teaspoon onion powder

¼ teaspoon gluten-free
Worcestershire sauce

Sea salt to taste

FOR THE SALAD:

1 head cos lettuce, chopped into
bite-size pieces

120g mixed salad leaves

125g cherry tomatoes, halved

1 ripe avocado, peeled,
stoned and diced

½ cucumber, diced

¼ small red onion, sliced

2 hard-boiled eggs,
peeled and chopped

2 tablespoons chopped
cooked bacon

1. First make the dressing: whisk all of the ingredients together in a mixing bowl. Season with salt and sprinkle with cayenne pepper if desired. Store in an airtight container in the fridge for up to 5 days.

2. Toss all of the ingredients in a salad bowl. Add the Dairy-Free Ranch Dressing, toss to coat, and serve.

TIP
You can play with different herbs and spices to create different flavours for the many ways you will use this dressing.

MIXED GREEN SALAD WITH SPROUTED SUNFLOWER SEED VINAIGRETTE

PI
DF
V

Serves 4–6

FOR THE SPROUTED SUNFLOWER SEED VINAIGRETTE:

100g raw, hulled, whole sunflower seeds, soaked in 720ml water for 6 hours or overnight (see Tip)

1 clove garlic

½ tablespoon peeled, finely chopped fresh ginger

1 tablespoon finely chopped fresh lemongrass or 1 teaspoon dried powdered lemongrass

180ml filtered water

4 tablespoons light miso paste

180ml extra virgin olive oil

1 tablespoon fresh lemon juice

Sea salt to taste

FOR THE SALAD:

300g mixed salad leaves

65g grated carrots

6 radishes, halved and thinly sliced

¼ cucumber, thinly sliced

1. First make the dressing: drain and rinse the sunflower seeds and put them in a high-powered blender. Add the garlic, ginger and lemongrass and run the blender for 1 minute. Add the filtered water and run for 30 seconds. Add the miso paste and lemon juice and run for 1 further minute. While the blender is running, slowly add the olive oil. Check the vinaigrette for salt. It may not need it depending on the saltiness of the miso.

2. Toss the greens and vegetables together in a salad bowl. Add the vinaigrette and toss to coat.

TIP

This is a simple green salad. What makes it special is the vinaigrette.

The sprouted sunflower seeds called for in this recipe are at the beginning of the sprouting process. You can take it further by returning the drained and rinsed seeds to the soaking container without water to sit for another 6–8 hours. This will create a more pronounced sprout with a light, artichoke-like flavour. Very often we soak the sprouted sunflower seeds like this, just to add them to salads on their own. After sprouting, they will keep for up to 5 days in the fridge.

RED CABBAGE & SWEET CARROT SLAW WITH GINGER VINAIGRETTE

There is a lot of grating required, which makes this recipe a bit of a workout for the biceps, so roll up your sleeves and get into it. What does make it convenient though, is that it keeps for several days, even if it's already dressed.

Serves 4–6

FOR THE GINGER VINAIGRETTE:

2 tablespoons peeled, finely chopped fresh ginger

2 teaspoons finely chopped garlic

3 tablespoons toasted sesame oil

4 tablespoons gluten-free tamari

3 tablespoons fresh lime juice

2 teaspoons raw honey

FOR THE SALAD:

½ head large red cabbage, cored and thinly sliced

½ head broccoli, stem removed, grated or shredded

1 carrot, grated

4 radishes, halved and thinly sliced

1 tablespoon sesame seeds

1. First make the dressing: put all of the ingredients in a small bowl and whisk them together.

2. Put all of the vegetables in a large bowl. Add the Ginger Vinaigrette and toss to coat the salad well. Garnish with the sesame seeds, wipe your brow and serve.

TIP

This is the ultimate potluck salad because it goes well with just about anything, both hot or cold, and people love it.

EASY-BREEZY MASSAGED KALE & AVOCADO SALAD

Kale is so beautiful and so healthy, yet some people find that eating it can feel like a lot of work. This recipe makes it tender, delicious and easy for the whole family to enjoy. Massaging the kale with lemon juice makes it easy to digest, so all of the vitamins and minerals are readily available to your body.

Serves 4–6

2 bunches curly kale

4 tablespoons fresh lemon juice

2–3 teaspoons sea salt

1 ripe avocado, peeled, stoned and diced

3 tablespoons extra virgin olive oil

1. Remove the ribs from the kale and cut the leaves into bite-size pieces. Put the leaves in a large mixing bowl.

2. Add the lemon juice, sea salt, avocado and olive oil to the kale. Get all up and personal with the kale, massaging it thoroughly to distribute the ingredients with your hands for approximately 10 minutes, until the leaves soften, darken in colour, shrink in size, and become a silky texture. (You may want to remove your jewellery for this part!)

3. Let the salad sit for approximately 20 minutes before serving to let all the flavours sink in.

TIP

Add your favourite salad add-ons, such as seared chicken, steak or fish to make this a meal in a bowl.

MEAT, FISH & POULTRY

Protein is an important part of any diet. The easiest way to get it is from nutritionally dense proteins like meat, fish and poultry, as well as eggs, nuts and seeds. Without enough protein, you can feel fatigued and your brainpower might be turned on to low volume. The quality of the meat you choose is important to getting the proper nutrients into your diet, too. See our sourcing page (page 120).

'FIND YOUR HERO'S JOURNEY
AND LIGHT UP THE PATH.'

PAN-SEARED FISH WITH CRISPY SKIN

Even in landlocked Boulder, Colorado, we love fish and can locally source a variety of lake trout. Find a fish that is available wild or sustainably farmed in your area. Serve these crisp-skinned fillets on top of salads, as a main feature to a vegetable dish or with your favourite style of eggs. We like the acidity of lemon or lime to add some piquant flavour.

Serves 4–6

4-6 × 140g boneless fish fillets, skin on (salmon, bass, trout or snapper)

2 tablespoons unsalted butter, ghee, coconut oil or extra virgin olive oil

Sea salt to taste

1 lemon, sliced, to serve

1. Use a sharp knife to score the skin side of each fillet with shallow incisions, not piercing the flesh. This will help prevent the skin from curling up.

2. Heat a large cast-iron frying pan or sauté pan to a medium to high heat. Add the fat to the pan (we prefer ghee) and salt both sides of the fish just before searing it.

3. Add the fish to the hot pan, skin side down, and let the skin crisp up and the flesh cook about two thirds of the way through, 3–5 minutes, depending on the thickness. You can baste the fish with the fat as it is cooking, but do not move it until it is ready to be flipped. (Coax it with a spatula to see if it is ready.)

4. Once the fish is cooked most of the way through and the skin is brown and crisp, flip the fish using a spatula. Cook flesh side down until just cooked through. This should only take a minute or two (see Tip).

5. Serve immediately with lemon slices alongside.

TIP
Keep an eye on the fish as you cook it, as overcooked fish loses its delicate flavour and can become more 'fishy' tasting and dry.

PAN-SEARED BONE-IN CHICKEN THIGHS

PI
DF

Properly searing chicken is a good technique to know for quick meals and as an addition to salads. You can use either dark meat or breasts. We prefer the legs and thighs because of their flavour and texture. We love to serve the leftovers cold for lunch the next day, over greens or on their own.

Serves 4–6

4–6 bone-in, skin-on free-range chicken thighs
Sea salt to taste
2 tablespoons extra virgin olive oil

1. Preheat the oven to 230°C/gas mark 8.

2. Generously season the chicken on both sides with salt.

3. Heat a large cast-iron frying pan or sauté pan to a medium-high heat. Add the olive oil. Put the chicken in the hot pan, skin-side down. Let the skin crisp up and brown, 4–6 minutes.

4. Flip the chicken so it is flesh side down in the pan and let it cook for a further 4–6 minutes, until lightly browned. Turn off the heat.

5. Cover the pan with aluminium foil and bake for 20–25 minutes. The chicken is done when it reaches an internal temperature of 74°C on a meat thermometer.

6. Let the chicken sit for 5 minutes before serving.

TIP
You can pan-sear breasts this way as well; just cut the oven-baking time to 10–12 minutes.

PAN-SEARED STEAK

We cook our meat to medium-rare, meaning pink on the inside. We find that the flavour and tenderness is best this way. In addition, it keeps some live enzymes intact to make the meat easier on your digestive system. This rosemary and garlic seasoned steak is great as a salad topper, alongside vegetable sides or for a hearty steak and eggs breakfast.

Serves 4–6

Sea salt

4–6 grass-fed steaks (rib-eye, flatiron, fillet, or sirloin), about 140g per person

4 tablespoons extra virgin olive oil

½ tablespoon fresh rosemary, chopped

½ tablespoon chopped shallots (optional)

½ teaspoon chopped garlic (optional)

15g unsalted butter (optional)

1. Salt the steaks generously, ideally about 30 minutes before cooking.

2. Heat a large cast-iron frying pan or sauté pan to a medium to high heat. Add the olive oil. Sear the steaks until they are a deep golden brown, then flip them and sear on the other side, 4–5 minutes per side. Reduce the heat to medium and cook the steaks until golden brown.

3. While the steak is cooking, add the rosemary to the pan along with the shallots and garlic, if using. If you are using the butter, add it to the pan, too, and baste the steak by spooning the butter over the top. Cook the steak until medium rare or desired temperature (see Tip).

4. Let the steak rest for 5–10 minutes to allow the juices to settle to maintain the moistness and flavour. Serve with a side of vegetables or a salad.

TIP
To cook the steak to your desired doneness, use a meat thermometer to measure the internal temperature:

Rare: 49°C
Medium-rare (perfect): 54°C
Medium: 60°C
Medium well: 65°C
Well: 71°C

SALMON
BURGER PATTIES

It's fun to change up your usual burger by using salmon instead of beef. Creating your own salmon burgers makes them more economical, plus you can get creative with the flavours. These tend to cook up best in a sauté pan, but they do also work well on the grill. Choosing sustainably farmed or wild salmon supports the proper treatment of seafood and it is high in healthful fats.

Makes eight 4-ounce servings

900g wild or sustainably farmed salmon fillets, skin and bones removed, cut into small dice

½ tablespoon capers, drained and finely chopped

ablespoons Whole-Egg Mayonnaise (page 98) or shop-bought mayo

1 tablespoon fresh lemon juice

75g Gluten-Free Breadcrumbs (page 99)

1 tablespoon finely chopped shallots

1 tablespoon finely chopped fresh dill

Sea salt to taste

2-3 tablespoons coconut oil

1. Put the diced salmon in large mixing bowl. Add the capers, mayonnaise, lemon juice, breadcrumbs, shallots and dill. Add a pinch of salt and mix well.

2. Divide the salmon mixture into 8 portions and form into patties.

3. Heat a large sauté pan over a medium heat and then melt enough of the coconut oil to cover the bottom of the pan.

4. When the oil is hot, put 2–4 patties in the pan, depending on the size of your pan. Cook for approximately 5 minutes before flipping the patties over. (Carefully test with a spatula to see if you can lift the burgers without sticking. If they are not easy to lift, wait another minute or two or add a little more oil.) Cook for 5 minutes on the other side, or until lightly browned. Transfer to a serving plate.

5. Add more coconut oil to the pan, if needed, and cook the remaining patties.

6. Serve these patties on a bed of rocket with lemon wedges and/or on a bun with our Tartare Sauce (page 100) or Sunflower Rocket Pesto (page 46).

TIP
Because fresh wild salmon is not available year-round, sometimes we buy it frozen. These salmon patties work out well when made with previously frozen wild salmon.

WHOLE-EGG MAYONNAISE

We love mayo! Growing up we enjoyed a lot of mayo on our sandwiches and even used it as a dip for cold chicken or turkey. It is easy to make and can be a healthy addition to your diet. With this recipe you avoid additives, preservatives and unhealthy oils that are in many of the shop-bought varieties.

Makes about 450g

1 whole egg plus 1 egg yolk, both at room temperature

1 tablespoon Dijon mustard

2 teaspoons sherry vinegar or white wine vinegar

1 tablespoon fresh lemon juice

420ml extra virgin olive oil or avocado oil

1. To a high-powered blender or food processor, add the egg and yolk, mustard, vinegar and lemon juice. Blend for 30 seconds.

2. With the blender or food processor running, very slowly begin to drizzle in the oil (a very slow drip is what's required here). Continue to add drip by drip until the mixture starts to emulsify and thicken. At this point, you can begin to pour the oil a bit faster until the mixture reaches a mayonnaise consistency. As soon as you have a mayonnaise consistency, stop processing.

3. The mayonnaise can be used immediately or refrigerated in a glass container for up to 5 days.

TIP

Mayonnaise can be flavoured in many different ways depending on how you are going to use it. We blend in roasted garlic, sun-dried tomatoes or basil pesto to name a few of our favourites.

HOMEMADE GLUTEN-FREE BREADCRUMBS

DF
V

Store-bought gluten-free breadcrumbs can be pricey. Why spend the money when they are so easy to make at home from leftover bread?

Makes about 150g

4-5 slices gluten-free bread, any kind

½ teaspoon sea salt (optional)

Dried seasonings, such as oregano and parsley, to taste (optional)

1. Preheat the oven to 160°C/gas mark 3.

2. Toast the bread on a baking sheet until dry and toasted, about 8–10 minutes flipping over once; let cool completely. Or dry out the bread on the kitchen counter, uncovered, overnight.

3. Break up the slices of dried bread into chunks, place in a food processor, and pulse until coarse crumbs form. Add the optional salt and seasonings, if using, and pulse again until combined, or until the crumbs reach the desired consistency. (We prefer coarser panko-style crumbs, but you may like to grind them fine.)

4. Transfer the breadcrumbs to the baking sheet and bake on the centre rack for another 5–10 minutes, stirring occasionally.

5. Cool on the baking sheet before transferring the crumbs to a freezer-safe container. Seal tightly and store in the fridge or freezer until ready to use.

TIP
The crumbs can be used directly from the fridge or freezer, without defrosting and will stay fresh in the fridge for about 5 days and months in the freezer.

FISH STICKS WITH TARTAR SAUCE

This crunchy finger food is a good way to get kids eating fish. Not only are they fun for dipping, they contain Omega-3s, which help brain development. Even the fish-averse adults in your life will enjoy these, especially with our Tangy Tartare Sauce for dipping.

Serves 4–6

675g firm white fish, skinned and deboned (we prefer cod)

60g brown rice flour

1 teaspoon sea salt

3 medium eggs

150g Gluten-Free Breadcrumbs (page 99)

2 tablespoons extra virgin olive oil

4–5 tablespoons coconut oil

Sea salt, to taste

Tangy Tartare Sauce (below), to serve

Lemon wedges, to garnish

1. Prepare your ingredients and arrange them in the following sequence near your hob: Cut the fish into wide strips, about 2.5cm × 7.5cm each. Mix the flour and salt on a large flat plate. Whisk the eggs in a large bowl. Mix the breadcrumbs and olive oil in another large bowl.

2. Individually coat each strip of fish in the flour mixture and set aside on a plate. When all of the fish is coated with flour, dip each piece individually in the egg wash, and then coat thoroughly in the breadcrumbs; set aside on a plate.

3. Heat a large sauté pan over medium-high heat. Add half of the coconut oil to the pan. When the oil is completely melted, place some of the coated fish strips in the pan. (Do not overcrowd the pan – you will need to cook in batches.) Cook for a few minutes on each side, until the fish strips have a nice golden brown colour. Transfer them to a kitchen paper-lined plate to drain. Repeat this step with the remaining coconut oil and fish sticks.

4. Serve the fish sticks hot with Tangy Tartare Sauce and wedges of lemon.

TIP

Another version of this recipe is to bake the fish sticks. It is easier but we find it doesn't have quite the crisp crust as the version with coconut oil. Preheat the oven to 200°C/gas mark 6. Coat the fish sticks as described in step 2. Arrange them on an ungreased baking sheet or in a large cast-iron frying pan, and bake for 20–25 minutes, flipping them over halfway through the cooking time, until golden brown on both sides.

TANGY TARTARE SAUCE

Makes about 225g

170g Whole-Egg Mayonnaise (page 98) or shop-bought

3 tablespoons finely diced dill pickles

1 tablespoon chopped capers

1 tablespoon chopped fresh dill

2 teaspoons fresh lemon juice

1 teaspoon raw apple cider vinegar

Sea salt to taste

This tangy sauce is a natural accompaniment to fish. It is fresh tasting and adds vibrancy and acidity to play beautifully as a spread or dipping sauce.

Stir together all of the ingredients in a mixing bowl. Store in an airtight container in the fridge for up to 5 days.

SEAFOOD STEW WITH BASIL PESTO

This is always part of our annual Christmas Eve family dinner. Our grandmother loved to make it with calamari and serve it over homemade pasta. There are many different kinds of seafood you can use here, so ask your fishmonger what is looking the best. This stew is versatile enough to serve as a fancy dinner or a simple meal. Present it over pasta, or serve it with warm, crusty gluten-free bread and your favourite bottle of wine.

Serves 4–6

2 tablespoons extra virgin olive oil

1 small onion, chopped

1 teaspoon fennel seeds

2 teaspoons dried oregano

2 cloves garlic, finely chopped

225g cleaned calamari, cut into 1cm rings (see Tip)

225g salmon fillets, skinned, boned and diced into small pieces

240ml dry white wine

2 tablespoons tomato purée

500g crushed canned tomatoes

225g uncooked large prawns, peeled and deveined

15g unsalted butter (optional)

Sea salt

4–6 teaspoons Fresh Basil Pesto (recipe below)

Freshly grated Pecorino Romano or Parmigiano-Reggiano cheese (optional)

1. Heat a medium-size saucepan over a medium heat and add 1 tablespoon of the olive oil. Add the onion, fennel seeds and oregano and cook for 2 minutes with the lid on. Take the lid off and cook for another 6 minutes, stirring frequently.

2. Add the garlic and cook for a further 2 minutes. Add the calamari and sauté for 3 minutes. Add the salmon and sauté for a further 3 minutes. Pour in the wine and reduce by half; this will take approximately 6 minutes.

3. Add the tomato purée and crushed tomatoes, cover with a lid and simmer the stew for 20 minutes to let the flavours blend together. Add the prawns and cook for a further 10 minutes.

4. Turn off the heat, add the butter, if using, and season with salt. Cover the pan and let the stew sit for 5 minutes before serving.

5. Top each serving with 1 teaspoon of Basil Pesto (recipe below) and the grated cheese of your choice.

TIP

For added tenderness, you can soak the calamari in milk for 2–6 hours before you cook it.

FRESH BASIL PESTO

This pesto brightens up almost any dish. Include a dollop on pastas, toast, meats, soups or roasted vegetables, or on our Baked Spaghetti Squash (page 126). This is a summertime go-to that tastes best with fresh picked, home-grown basil.

Makes about 240ml

50g fresh basil leaves

45g pine nuts, lightly toasted in a dry pan

1–2 cloves garlic, finely chopped

Sea salt

35g freshly grated Pecorino Romano cheese

120ml extra virgin olive oil

1. Put the basil leaves, toasted pine nuts and garlic in the bowl of a food processor and pulse for 30 seconds. Add a pinch of salt. Add the Pecorino and process for a further 30 seconds, scraping down the sides of the bowl as needed. With the food processor running, slowly drizzle in the olive oil and then season with salt.

2. Serve immediately or store for up to 3 days in a tightly covered glass container.

TIP

We love using basil pesto as a salad dressing, especially with roasted veg. To make pesto into a vinaigrette, whisk in olive oil and a touch of balsamic vinegar until the pesto is thinned and you have the flavour you want.

CHICKEN FINGERS

Serves 4 kids or 2 adults

450g boneless free-range chicken thighs

2 medium eggs

Sea salt to taste

100g Gluten-Free Breadcrumbs (page 99)

1 teaspoon garlic powder

1 teaspoon onion powder

3 tablespoons coconut oil or extra virgin olive oil

Dairy-Free Ranch Dressing (page 82), to serve

1. Prepare your ingredients and arrange them in the following sequence near your hob: Lightly pound the chicken thighs and cut them into approximately 5cm-wide strips. In a shallow dish, lightly beat the eggs with a dash of salt. In another shallow dish, stir together the breadcrumbs, garlic powder, onion powder and a dash of salt.

2. Dip the chicken strips into the eggs, allowing the excess to drain off, and then dip them into the breadcrumbs, ensuring that you coat them thoroughly. Set aside on a large plate.

3. Heat 1 1/2 tablespoons of the coconut oil in a large sauté pan or griddle over a medium heat.

4. Add half of the chicken strips to the pan and cook, flipping them at least once, until they are golden brown on both sides and cooked through, about 15 minutes total. Transfer to a plate layered with kitchen paper to drain.

5. After the first batch is done, wipe the pan with kitchen paper. Reheat the pan over a medium heat with the remaining coconut oil and cook the rest of the chicken strips.

6. Serve with a side of our ranch dressing for dipping.

TIP
For an egg-free version, substitute 3 tablespoons canned full-fat coconut milk and 1 tablespoon olive oil per egg.

DAIRY-FREE FRIED CHICKEN

DF

Serves 4–6

1.4 litres filtered water

120g sea salt

1.35 – 1.8kg bone-in chicken pieces

1 × 400g can full-fat coconut milk

½ tablespoon apple cider vinegar

240g brown rice flour

80g potato or tapioca flour

1 teaspoon sea salt, plus more for seasoning the chicken

2 teaspoons garlic powder

2 teaspoons paprika

2 teaspoons cayenne pepper

120ml coconut oil

120ml extra virgin olive oil

1. In a large bowl, combine the water and salt, stirring until the salt dissolves. Add the chicken pieces to the brine and refrigerate for 2–8 hours. (We usually put chicken in to brine in the morning before work begins.)

2. When you're ready to fry the chicken, preheat the oven to 180°C/gas mark 4. Drain the chicken and thoroughly pat it dry with kitchen paper.

3. In a mixing bowl, whisk together the coconut milk and vinegar. In another mixing bowl, mix together the flours, salt, garlic powder, paprika and cayenne pepper.

4. Working with one piece at a time, dip the chicken into the canned coconut milk and let the excess drip off as well as you can. Dip the chicken into the flour mixture (you can double-dip for a thicker coating). Set the prepared pieces aside on a large plate.

5. Heat a large sauté pan to a medium heat. Add 4 tablespoons of each of the oils, heat until lightly bubbling, and add 3–4 pieces of chicken to the pan. Fry the chicken on each side for 6 minutes or until deep golden brown. Drain on kitchen paper.

6. Working in two to four batches total, fry the rest of the chicken, ensuring that you strain or wipe out any burnt or crusty bits in between batches and to add more of the oil when needed.

7. When all of the chicken has been fried and drained, put it into a large baking dish and bake for approximately 25 minutes, until it reaches an internal temperature of 74°C on a meat thermometer.

8. Let sit for 5 minutes and serve. We enjoy this with Nelson's Buttermilk Drop Scones on the side.

TIP

After lots of experimentation, we chose to first fry and then bake this chicken to get the full flavour and crispy effect without fully submerging the chicken in oil. Not only does this method deliver the best taste and texture, it also makes less of a mess in the kitchen. This can also be prepared with buttermilk instead of the coconut milk and vinegar mixture, if you prefer.

WHOLE ROASTED CHICKEN WITH MAPLE-ROASTED VEGETABLES

This is a recipe that we hope will become one of your family favourites. The house smells so delicious, and it is a dish that is easy to love by the whole family. The sweet fruit and vegetables contrast nicely with the savoury chicken.

PI
DF

Serves 4–6

2 tablespoons extra virgin olive oil
or 30g softened unsalted butter
(optional)

Sea salt

1.8kg free-range roasting chicken
(see Tip)

2 lemons, halved

3 cloves garlic

5 rosemary sprigs

2 tablespoons raw
apple cider vinegar

360ml chicken stock (to make your
own, see page 64)

1 ½ tablespoons maple syrup

15g unsalted butter (optional)

3 apples (we like Honeycrisp or Fuji),
peeled, cored and cut into cubes

3 carrots, peeled and cut
into large dice

1 large sweet potato, peeled
and cut into large dice

½ onion, sliced

½ bulb fennel, sliced

1. Preheat the oven to 200°C/gas mark 6.

2. Rub the olive oil and a generous amount of salt on the chicken. Put the lemon, garlic and rosemary into the cavity of the chicken and set aside.

3. In a small saucepan, combine the vinegar, stock, maple syrup, butter, if using, and a healthy pinch of salt. Cook over a medium heat until reduced by half.

4. In the bottom of a roasting tin or Dutch oven, arrange the apples, carrots, sweet potato, onion and fennel to form a bed for the chicken. Pour the chicken stock mixture over the vegetables and lightly toss. Place the prepared chicken on top of the vegetables.

5. Roast the chicken for 1 hour 30 minutes to 2 hours, until it reaches an internal temperature of 74°C on a meat thermometer.

6. Transfer the chicken to a serving plate and let it rest for 15 minutes. Carve the chicken and serve it over the maple-roasted vegetables.

TIP

To calculate the roasting time for a larger or smaller bird, estimate 22–25 minutes per 450g. Even after a free-range chicken is roasted, the bones can be used to make stock. Just follow our Chicken Bone Broth recipe on page 64; the only difference is you may want to simmer the bones for a couple of hours longer in order to pull out all of the nutrients and flavour.

BARB-ECK-QUE CHICKEN

Serves 4–6

8 - 10 bone-in, skin-on free-range chicken thighs

4 tablespoons extra virgin olive oil

4 tablespoons Eck's Dry Rub (recipe below)

240ml Barbecue Sauce (recipe below)

1. Preheat an outdoor gas or charcoal grill to a low heat. Scrape the hot grill plates clean with a wire brush so the chicken will cook without sticking.

2. Brush the chicken thighs lightly with the olive oil. Sprinkle the dry rub very liberally all over the thighs.

3. Grill the chicken thighs, turning and brushing them liberally with the barbecue sauce every 5 minutes or so, until the skin is super crisp and the barbecue sauce is syrupy and caramelised, 40–45 minutes total. (Using a meat thermometer, check to ensure the internal temperature of the chicken has reached 74°C before removing the chicken from the grill; see Tip.)

4. Let the chicken sit for 5 minutes before serving.

TIP

As Eck always says, the way to make really yummy barbecue chicken is to cook the thighs low and slow. This brings out their flavour and makes them super-tender.

BARBECUE SAUCE

Makes about 240ml

1 × 400g can tomatoes, drained

2½ tablespoons molasses

1 tablespoon raw honey

2 tablespoons apple cider vinegar

¼ teaspoon dried oregano

¼ teaspoon garlic powder

¼ teaspoon mustard powder

1. Purée the tomatoes in a blender.

2. Transfer the tomatoes to a saucepan, add the remaining ingredients and simmer for 10 minutes, stirring occasionally.

Jennifer: *This was the dish my husband,* Eric (Eck) made when my whole family came over for the first time after we were married. Coming from a big Italian family, I am very used to big meals and chaos. Eck put so much love and time into this dish that my family was hooked not only on the chicken but on my hubby as well. To this day, you'll find him standing over the grill in the summertime when the whole family gets together at our place. He is very proud of this dish and was over the moon about having it included in our cookery book.

ECK'S DRY RUB

Makes about 120ml

4 tablespoons smoked paprika

1 tablespoon garlic powder

2 teaspoons sea salt

1 teaspoon cumin

1 teaspoon cayenne pepper

¼ teaspoon mustard powder

Combine all ingredients in a bowl. Store in a tightly sealed glass jar.

SAUSAGE AND PEPPERS

Growing up in an expressive Italian family, many stories were told over sausages and peppers. It was a quick and easy dinner Dad would throw on the hob so the focus could be on family time instead of slaving over a hot stove. Serve straight out of the oven with yummy, crusty Italian bread on the side.

Serves 4–6

2 tablespoons extra virgin olive oil

8 Italian-style sausages

1 large onion, sliced

Sea salt to taste

2 large red peppers, seeded and sliced

100g mushrooms, sliced

2 cloves garlic, finely chopped

1. Preheat the oven to 160°C/gas mark 3.

2. Heat a large sauté pan over a medium heat for 2 minutes and then add the olive oil.

3. Add the sausages and cook, turning frequently, covering the pan to avoid splatter, until the sausages are browned on all sides, approximately 10 minutes. Set aside on a plate.

4. To the same pan, add the onion and a pinch of salt and cook for about 4 minutes, until translucent. Add the peppers and mushrooms and sauté until soft, approximately 8 minutes. Add the garlic and sauté for a further 2 minutes, stirring occasionally.

5. Transfer the mixed vegetables to a large baking dish (38cm × 28cm is ideal) and top with the sausages. Bake for approximately 30 minutes to allow all of the flavours and juices to mingle. Serve straight out of the oven.

TIP

Sausages and peppers make great leftovers. Try them on sandwiches or over pasta.

SEARED PORK CHOPS WITH BRAISED CABBAGE AND FENNEL

Serves 4–6

Sea salt

4-6 × 170g bone-in shoulder blade or centre cut chops (see Tip)

2 tablespoons extra virgin olive oil, if needed

¼ onion, thinly sliced

½ teaspoon caraway seeds

½ large fennel bulb or 1 small bulb, cored and thinly sliced

½ large cabbage, cored and thinly sliced

480ml chicken stock (to make your own, see page 64)

10 sprigs fresh dillweed

3-4 slices bacon (optional)

1. Preheat the oven to 150°C/gas mark 2.

2. Generously salt the pork chops on both sides.

3. Heat the olive oil in a Dutch oven or heavy-based pan to a medium-high heat. Sear the chops on both sides until browned, approximately 4 minutes per side. Set the chops aside on a large plate, leaving the fat in the pan.

4. If more oil is needed, add the olive oil to the pan, then add the onion and caraway seeds and sauté until the onion is soft and translucent. Add the fennel and sauté until soft, then add the cabbage and sauté until soft. Season the cabbage mixture with salt.

5. Pour in the stock and return the pork to the pan. Top each pork chop with dill sprigs and bacon strips, if using. Cover and braise for 1 hour 30 minutes, until tender.

6. Chop the bacon. Remove and discard the dill sprigs. Serve the pork and cabbage immediately, topped with the bacon.

TIP
There are many cuts of pork you could use for this dish, however, we recommend bone-in because it has the best flavour and adds flavour to the cabbage and stock as well. We like to serve this with Apple Pear Purée (page 124) on the side.

BEAN-FREE CHILLI

Serves 4–6

2 tablespoons extra virgin olive oil

½ small onion, medium diced

2 green peppers, seeded and medium diced

1 poblano chilli, medium diced

1 yellow or green courgette, medium diced

50g mushrooms, sliced

2 cloves garlic, finely chopped

1.1kg grass-fed minced beef

4 tablespoons chilli powder

1 tablespoon ground cumin

240ml chicken stock (to make your own, see page 64)

800g canned diced tomatoes

3 tablespoons chopped coriander, to serve (optional)

Soured cream, to serve

Fresh lime wedges, to serve

Sea salt to taste

1. Heat a large, heavy-based pan over a medium heat and add 1 tablespoon of the olive oil.

2. Add the onions and sauté for 4 minutes. Add the green peppers and poblano chilli; sauté for 4 minutes. Add the remaining 1 tablespoon olive oil along with the courgette, garlic and mushrooms; sauté for 4 minutes. Add the beef, chilli powder and cumin; sauté for 4 minutes. Stir in the chicken stock and diced tomatoes, cover the pan, and simmer on a low heat for 45 minutes, until the flavours are blended. Add sea salt to taste.

5. Garnish with coriander, soured cream and lime wedges and serve.

 TIP
You can get very creative with the vegetables as long as you keep the peppers called for in this recipe. Leftovers can be frozen in an airtight container for up to 2 months.

Jessica: This is a quick, easy recipe that is very satisfying on cold autumn and winter nights. Both of my kids eat it voraciously, which makes me happy because it is a quick preparation and an easy cleanup!

GRASS-FED BEEF STEW

This is a nourishing, hearty dish that is extremely warming during the winter months, we enjoy it as a après ski meal in front of a fire to replenish energy and to warm our bones. This stew is also a hit for casual entertaining and easily scales up for big-batch cooking.

Serves 4–6

2 tablespoons extra virgin olive oil or coconut oil

1 small yellow onion, chopped

Sea salt to taste

675g grass-fed beef or buffalo stew meat, cut into 2.5cm cubes

2 tablespoons gluten-free Worcestershire sauce

75g mushrooms, sliced

1 or 2 cloves garlic, finely chopped

120ml sherry or red wine

1 ½ teaspoons ground nutmeg

1 teaspoon fennel seeds

3–4 thyme sprigs

2 rosemary sprigs

1.2 litres beef or chicken stock (to make your own, see page 63)

2 small carrots, peeled and diced

2 celery sticks, peeled and diced

small sweet potato, peeled and diced

2 tablespoons tapioca or arrowroot flour

15g unsalted butter, optional

1. Heat a heavy casserole pan over a medium to high heat and add the oil and onion. Cook until soft, approximately 5 minutes. Season with salt. Add the beef and cook for approximately 5 minutes, until browned.

2. Add the Worcestershire sauce and mushrooms and cook for 5 minutes until the mushrooms are cooked through. Add the garlic and cook for 2 minutes, stirring occasionally.

3. Add the sherry or red wine and reduce the liquid by half, then add the nutmeg, fennel seeds, thyme, rosemary and the stock. Bring to the boil.

2. Add the carrots, celery and sweet potato, reduce the heat to a simmer, and cook with the lid on for 15 minutes, until the vegetables are tender. Remove the lid and cook over a medium heat for a further 15 minutes (this will start the evaporation and thickening process).

3. Add the flour to a measuring cup or bowl. Mix in a few tablespoons of the beef stock until the flour is completely dissolved. Add the flour slurry to the pan and cook over a medium-low heat for approximately 1 hour 30 minutes, until the flavours are blended.

4. Turn off the heat. Stir in the butter if using and let the stew sit for 10 minutes with the lid on.

5. Divide among bowls and serve immediately. Leftovers can be stored in an airtight container in the fridge for up to 5 days.

TIP

We like to serve this stew over Cauliflower Mash (page 128) or on its own with crusty gluten free bread or Nelson's Buttermilk Drop Scones (page 40). You can replace the sherry or red wine with additional stock if preferred.

DAD'S POT OF SAUCE WITH MEATBALLS

If using spaghetti squash

Whenever we go back home to New Jersey, this is what Dad prepares on our first night. The scent of this sauce is home to us. It is hearty, healing and nourishing and represents family, love, indulgence and our Jersey Italian heritage. We enjoy opening a nice bottle of red wine, settling back in with our brother and parents and catching up on each other's lives. Now watching the kids devour the sauce and meatballs feels full circle. Home really is where the heart is. Thanks for this one, Dad.

Serves 4–6

2 tablespoons extra virgin olive oil
1 medium onion, chopped
1 red pepper, seeded and chopped
3 cloves garlic, finely chopped
800g canned diced tomatoes
450g canned crushed tomatoes
2 teaspoons dried oregano
Sea salt to taste
100g chestnut mushrooms, sliced
2 tablespoons tomato purée
Dad's Meatballs (below)
2 tablespoons chopped fresh basil

1. Heat a large saucepan over a medium-high heat and add the olive oil. Add the onion and pepper, reduce the heat to medium and sauté for 8 minutes, until the onion begins to turn translucent. Add the garlic and cook for a further 2–3 minutes, stirring frequently.

2. Stir in the diced and crushed tomatoes, oregano and salt. Let simmer for approximately 15 minutes.

3. Add the mushrooms and the tomato purée to the pan. Cover and cook for a further 30–45 minutes, stirring occasionally.

4. Add the meatballs, cover the pan, and continue to cook for a further 30 minutes. Add the fresh basil 10 minutes before you plan on serving the sauce.

TIP
Both the sauce and the meatballs can be made in bigger batches and kept frozen. You can freeze the meatballs right along with the sauce and heat them back up together in a pan over a medium heat.

DAD'S MEATBALLS

Makes approximately 10 meatballs

450g grass-fed minced beef (we prefer 85 per cent lean for juiciness)
2 cloves garlic, finely chopped
10g fresh parsley, chopped
20g Pecorino Romano cheese, grated
45g ground flaxseeds (flaxseed meal)
1 medium egg
1 teaspoon sea salt
2–3 tablespoons extra virgin olive oil

1. In a large mixing bowl, combine the beef, garlic, parsley, cheese, flaxseeds, egg and salt, using your hands to mix all the ingredients together.

2. Form the minced beef mixture into approximately 10 meatballs, allowing about 2 heaped tablespoons for each.

3. Heat a large sauté pan over a medium-high heat. Add the olive oil. Sauté the meatballs on all sides to brown them evenly, about 8–10 minutes total.

4. Add the meatballs to the Pot of Sauce and cook for a further 30 minutes, as described in step 4 of the recipe above (see Tip).

TIP
The meatballs will still be undercooked when you add them to the sauce. They will finish cooking in the sauce. If you are making them without the sauce, finish by baking the meatballs in a preheated 190°C/gas mark 5 oven for a further 15 minutes.

BRAISED SHORT RIBS

When we think of nourishing comfort food, this is one of the first recipes that comes to mind. We found that adding port wine contributes a hint of sweetness to the earthy flavour. (The alcohol cooks off during the cooking.) This is a sure-fire crowd pleaser for parties or big family gatherings and is especially delicious served with our Cauliflower Mash (page 128).

Serves 4–6

2 tablespoons extra virgin olive oil

2.3kg bone-in grass-fed beef short ribs

Sea salt to taste

2 carrots, chopped

2 sticks celery, diced

1 onion, chopped

360ml port wine

360ml red wine

1.2 litres beef or chicken stock (to make your own, see page 63), plus more if needed

4 thyme sprigs

4 rosemary sprigs

2 cloves garlic, finely chopped

15g unsalted butter (optional)

1. Preheat the oven to 160°C/gas mark 3.

2. In a large Dutch oven, heat the olive oil over a high heat until shimmering. Season the short ribs with a generous amount of salt. Add the short ribs to the hot pan and sear until all sides are deeply caramelised. Set aside on a serving plate.

3. Add the carrots, celery and onion to the pan juices in the Dutch oven along with a dash of salt. Sauté over a medium heat until the vegetables are caramelised and golden brown. Transfer the vegetables to the same serving plate as the short ribs.

4. Deglaze the pan with half the wine and half the port and reduce the liquid by half.

5. Return the short ribs and cooked vegetables to the Dutch oven. Add the stock, thyme, rosemary and garlic. The liquid should cover most of the ribs. If not, add more stock or water. Cover the pan with a lid and bake in the oven for 2 hours and thirty minutes, until the ribs are tender.

6. Remove the pan from the oven and transfer the ribs to a serving plate to rest. Strain the cooking liquid into a pan and reduce by half over a medium heat to thicken into a sauce.

7. Remove the sauce from the heat. Stir in the butter, if using and season with sea salt if necessary. Serve the short ribs with the sauce poured over.

TIP

This recipe can also be made with bone-in lamb, pork or buffalo. If you choose to prepare this recipe without wine or port, you can use additional stock instead.

Where Did You Come From? The Importance of Sourcing Your Food

For us humans, where a person comes from, what their upbringing was like, and how they were raised strongly influences how they view the world and how they interact with other people and with their environment. It is the same for fruits, vegetables and meats: where they come from and how they were grown dictates how they taste and, just as importantly, what they are made of; that is, their nutritional content. As we have mentioned before, your food literally becomes you. It is broken down in your body, enters through your cell walls and fuels every part of you. So, don't you want to know where your food comes from and how it was grown?

An apple often is not just an apple, as it can have up to 30 pesticides lurking on its skin and within its flesh. Whatever is on and in the food is also ingested by you. If there are pesticides on your vegetables, even if you scrub them, only some of the chemicals are removed. Pesticides can poison our insides, not to mention pollute our outside environment, including water sources and the air we breathe. These poisons have been proven to cause many different illnesses. We may not be able to control the air we breathe, but we can control what food we decide to put into our bodies.

Many factory-farmed meats contain antibiotics and hormones. Antibiotics are given to animals living in unsanitary, cramped conditions to combat disease, and hormones are given to make them grow faster and to increase milk production in cattle. Not only is this inhumane for the animals, but we are also ingesting these hormones and antibiotics as we eat the meat and drink the milk. The same goes for most farmed fish, where pesticides and antibiotics are often sprayed on the fish to kill bacteria, disease and parasites before the fish reaches the shop. It pollutes our oceans and harms marine life. Not sounding too appetising now, is it?

We highly recommend using local and organic ingredients whenever possible. Not only do these foods have the highest amount of vitamins, minerals, and more nutritional value and flavour, but they also support your local farmers and grocers and help build a sustainable ecosystem for your community.

Another huge factor in healthy sourcing of ingredients is choosing grass-fed meats. Why grass fed? The way animals are fed has a big effect on the nutrient composition of the meat. In their natural settings, animals such as cows, sheep and bison live on a healthy diet of grasses. Most intensely farmed animals are started out on grass and then finished on grain. When these animals are fed grain, they are forced to eat a food that is not part of their natural diet. This causes stress on their bodies and they may be less healthy.

A grass-finished animal is higher in nutrients, especially Omega-3s, which are very healthy for our bodies. Thus, eating grass-fed meat is incredibly nutritious. It is usually more expensive than its grain fed counterpart. If this is a concern, you can purchase less expensive grass-fed cuts and cook them lower and longer in stews and roasts. You may also find a farm in your area that sells animals by the half or quarter; an economical way to purchase meat. There is a flavour difference, too: Grass-fed meat has a more concentrated, cleaner flavour than grain-fed. It is also leaner, so when we're searing or grilling a grass-fed steak, we prefer to cook it to no more than medium-rare unless we'll be braising it afterwards.

We feel it is very important to use free range or even organic chicken if you can find it. Factory farmed, commercial birds are cooped up to where they can't move much at all, they are being fed unnatural sources of food and not only is it inhumane, but it changes the composition of the chickens and the nutritional value. Free range are healthier birds that can wander, be in sunlight and eat more natural forms of feed like insects and leftover crop. Free range, however, can also be fed the same unnatural feed as factory farmed birds, but organic chickens are fed certified organic feed so it ensures the best meat possible. Free range and organic chickens are higher in omega 3 fatty acids and Vitamins A and E. They are all around healthier for them and for you. So as we talk about, 'you are what you eat', it is good to keep in mind that you are also ingesting what your cows, fish, and chickens are ingesting, so be mindful of it as part of sourcing your animal proteins.

To understand your food and how it translates in your body is to empower yourself and truly thrive. Food is multidimensional in that it nourishes the mind, body and heart on both a physical and emotional level.

VEGGIE SIDES & MAINS

We love having snack foods on hand to munch on throughout the day that are substantial enough to keep us energised. We also have a lot of people coming into the restaurant who want to 'graze', trying a little bit of everything and the small dishes in this chapter are among their favourites. These also serve as creative components alongside our seared meats and other mains. In keeping with a Paleo-inspired way of eating, we've included many fun 'alternative' recipes that replace grains with vegetables. It keeps things nutritious and delicious!

APPLE PEAR PUREE

When we were kids, apple picking was a favourite way to spend the day with our many aunties and cousins. Our mum was one of 12 kids, so we had an abundance of both. We used to pile into the estate car with the hatchback down and scope out the best trees, then we'd pick and picnic all day long. We had apples for weeks, so we would get creative with recipes and this purée is one of our favourites. We loved it as a snack or a side. For this recipe, we like to use the sweeter apples, such as Gala, Honeycrisp or Fuji.

Makes about 700ml

4 large apples, peeled, cored and chopped into about 8 pieces

2 large ripe pears, peeled, cored and chopped into about 8 pieces

240ml apple juice or water (see Tip)

2 teaspoons fresh lemon juice

1 teaspoon ground cinnamon

¼ teaspoon ground nutmeg

1 teaspoon vanilla extract (to make your own, see page 171)

1. In a heavy-based pan over a medium-low heat, combine all the ingredients and cook for about 25 minutes, stirring occasionally. Transfer to a blender and purée until smooth.

2. Serve either warm or cold. The purée will keep in the fridge, stored in an airtight container, for 5–7 days.

TIP
The apple juice or water will only cover the bottom of the pan. It is used to steam the apples and pears; most of it will evaporate during cooking.

GRILLED BROCCOLI WITH LEMON

Growing up, we'd often spend the summer on the New Jersey shore with our many cousins – our extended family would rent multiple houses on the same street. In the evenings, we would wheel the grills down the street to one house so we had enough grill space to cook for everybody. There was a lot of laughter and a lot of cheap beer. This broccoli was a quick and easy green addition to all of the meat and seafood. It is also a wonderful addition to salads.

Serves 4–6

2 heads broccoli

4 tablespoons extra virgin olive oil

1 ½ tablespoons balsamic vinegar

3 tablespoons fresh lemon juice

Sea salt to taste

1. Preheat the grill to medium or medium-high.

2. Meanwhile, prepare the broccoli by cutting off about three-quarters of the stems and cutting each head into large florets. It is important to keep these pieces large enough so that they don't quickly burn or fall through the grill grate.

3. Mix together the oil, vinegar, lemon juice and salt in a large mixing bowl. Add the broccoli and toss to coat.

4. Transfer the broccoli to the grill, reserving the remaining dressing. Grill on all sides until the broccoli is lightly charred and softened, 10–15 minutes (see Tip).

5. Return the grilled broccoli to the mixing bowl and toss with the reserved dressing to coat. Chop the broccoli into smaller florets and serve.

TIP
It is okay for the broccoli to get darker, and even charred, in some places. This adds to the grilled flavour.

BAKED SPAGHETTI SQUASH

Squash is full of antioxidants, low in carbs, and results in glowing skin. This dish is a great Paleo alternative to pasta and will play well with your favourite pasta sauces.

Serves 4–6

1 spaghetti squash

2 tablespoons extra virgin olive oil

Sea salt to taste

1. Preheat the oven to 220°C/gas mark 7.

2. Cut off the stem end of the spaghetti squash, cut open and scoop out the seeds. Drizzle each half with the olive oil and sprinkle with salt.

3. Place the squash, flesh-side down, on a baking sheet, and bake for approximately 45 minutes. Let cool slightly.

4. Using a fork, scrape the spaghetti squash strands into a bowl. Serve warm as an alternative to pasta, or as a side dish with butter or more olive oil and salt.

TIP

We love sautéing wild mushrooms, garlic, tomatoes and sage and then adding the squash for a simple and delicious fall dish.

CAULIFLOWER MASHERS

A Paleo alternative to mashed potatoes, this is a Shine favourite that we serve with stews and as a side with meat or fish. If you leave out the rosemary, it makes a nourishing baby food as well.

Serves 4–6

1 large head cauliflower, broken into florets

1 tablespoon coconut oil

1 teaspoon chopped rosemary

2 tablespoons nutritional yeast

Sea salt to taste

1. Bring 480ml water to the boil in a large sauté pan. Add the cauliflower, cover and steam for approximately 12 minutes. The cauliflower is done when you can pierce it with a fork.

2. Drain the cauliflower, reserving 240ml of the cooking water (see Tip). Pour the reserved water and cauliflower into a food processor and process until smooth.

3. Add the coconut oil, rosemary, nutritional yeast and salt and process until fully incorporated. Store in the fridge in an airtight container for up to 5 days.

TIP
If you like a thicker consistency, add less liquid. For additional flavour, you can substitute chicken stock for the water.

CAULIFLOWER RICE

A Paleo alternative to rice, this has a very similar texture and holds juices and flavours really well. We love serving it with roasted veg, as a side dish to any protein, with eggs or anywhere else you would use rice.

Makes 500g

1 head cauliflower, outer leaves removed

1 tablespoon extra virgin olive oil or coconut oil or 15g butter

Sea salt to taste

1. Using your hands, break apart the cauliflower into large florets. Chop the core into smaller pieces.

2. Working in two or three batches, process the cauliflower for 30 seconds, stopping to mix in the larger pieces. Continue for 2–3 minutes until the cauliflower resembles small pieces of rice. Repeat with the remaining batches. At this point, the rice can be eaten raw (see Tip), or proceed with the cooking instructions below.

3. Heat a large pan over a medium heat. Add the oil and sauté the cauliflower rice for 10–12 minutes, stirring frequently, until the rice is softened and cooked through.

4. Stir in salt to taste and serve immediately, or store in the fridge for up to 5 days.

TIP
Add raw Cauliflower Rice to salads and soups for additional crunch.

CAULIFLOWER FRIED RICE

This is our cauliflower rice taken to another dimension. The additional vegetables make it a satisfying vegetarian main dish. Tamari is almost always gluten-free (check the bottle!), is less salty than typical soy sauce, and can be used in place of it in any recipe.

Serves 4

2 tablespoons coconut oil or olive oil

3 medium eggs, whisked

60g carrots, finely chopped

2 tablespoons finely chopped yellow onion

50g green beans or frozen peas, chopped

50g mushrooms chopped (we like to use shiitakes)

500g Cauliflower Rice (page 129)

4 tablespoons gluten-free tamari

2 tablespoons toasted sesame oil

4 tablespoons thinly sliced spring onions

Sea salt to taste

1. In a large sauté pan over a low-medium heat, heat 1 tablespoon coconut oil. Pour in the whisked eggs, swirling them slightly to get a thin even layer on the bottom of the pan. Continue to cook until just cooked through. Slide the cooked eggs onto a chopping board and chop into small dice. Set aside.

2. Increase the heat to medium-high and add the remaining tablespoon of coconut oil to the pan. Add the carrots and sauté for 4–5 minutes. Add the onion, green beans and mushrooms and sauté for 5 minutes. Add the cauliflower rice and cook for a further 5 minutes, stirring frequently, until lightly browned and cooked through. Add the tamari and mix well for 1 minute.

3. Turn off the heat and add the sesame oil, reserved cooked eggs, and spring onions. Mix well, add salt to taste and serve.

TIP
Cooked minced beef or turkey can be added with the eggs and spring onions to make this a hearty main dish.

PARSNIP CHIPS

A fun way to get to know parsnips is to make them into chips. They are more nutritionally dense than potatoes, but still hold a similar consistency. On their own, parsnips have a nice warming spiced flavour but also take on additional flavours well. Cooking them to the point they are brown on the outside but soft on the inside makes for a very satisfying Paleo alternative to potato chips.

Serves 4–6

3 tablespoons extra virgin olive oil

2 tablespoons chopped fresh parsley

8 medium parsnips, peeled and cut into chips

Sea salt to taste

Truffle oil, for drizzling (optional)

1. Preheat the oven to 200°C/gas mark 6.

2. Whisk together the olive oil and parsley in a mixing bowl. Add the parsnip chips, toss to coat, and season with salt.

3. Spread the chips out on a large baking sheet. Bake for 15 minutes, or until the chips are lightly browned on one side.

4. Remove from the oven and flip the chips over with a large spatula. Increase the oven temperature to 230°C/gas mark 8. Bake for a further 5 minutes until crisp and lightly browned on both sides.

5. Serve hot, drizzled with truffle oil, if using, or with your favourite dipping sauce (see Tip).

TIP

These chips are great dipped in our Dairy-Free Ranch Dressing (page 82), Rocket Sunflower Pesto (page 46) or even our Whole-Egg Mayonnaise (page 98).

CHOPPED ROASTED VEGGIES

These vegetables are packed with flavour and make a great accompaniment to any main dish or your salad greens. We also like to use them as part of an antipasti plate with meats and cheeses.

Makes about 500g

2½ tablespoons extra virgin olive oil

1½ teaspoons maple syrup

1½ teaspoons balsamic vinegar

¼ teaspoon dried oregano

500g assorted chopped vegetables in 2.5cm pieces (asparagus, onion, parsnips, mushrooms, swede, green courgettes, yellow courgettes, halved small cherry tomatoes are all great options)

Sea salt to taste

1. Preheat the oven to 190°C/gas mark 5.

2. Whisk together the oil, maple syrup, vinegar and oregano in a small bowl.

3. Put the chopped vegetables in a large bowl. Pour the dressing over the vegetables and stir to coat.

4. Spread out the veg in a roasting tin and bake uncovered for 30 minutes, stirring once during the cooking time. Season with salt.

5. Serve hot or at room temperature.

TIP
This recipe is versatile. You can use almost any vegetables you have on hand, or whatever you find in season at your local market.

'CREAMED' KALE

This is our dairy-free take on creamed spinach. We took out the cream and added cashews, miso and nutritional yeast to make it a super-nutritious and delicious side dish. We enjoy this served with any grilled or seared seafood or on its own for a hearty protein-rich vegan dish.

Serves 4–6

2 large bunches of curly kale, de-stemmed and chopped into bite-size pieces (see Tip)

2 tablespoons fresh lemon juice

Sea salt to taste

120ml vegetable stock

¼ onion, finely chopped

1 clove garlic, finely chopped

360ml full-fat canned coconut milk

90g raw cashews, covered in water and simmered for 30 minutes, then drained

4 tablespoons nutritional yeast

2 tablespoons white miso

Pinch of freshly grated nutmeg

½ tablespoon coconut oil

1. Put the chopped kale in a mixing bowl with the lemon juice and a pinch of salt. Rub the kale between your hands for a few minutes, massaging the leaves until they have a silky texture. Set aside.

2. Heat the stock in a small pan over a medium heat. Add the onion and garlic and cook until softened, 5–7 minutes.

3. Transfer the seasoned stock to a blender or food processor. Add the coconut milk, cashews, nutritional yeast, miso and nutmeg and purée until smooth.

4. In a medium sauté pan, heat the coconut oil and sauté the kale until fully cooked. Add the coconut milk mixture and reduce until the sauce has thickened.

5. Serve immediately. The final product should be loose but not soupy.

TIP
Spinach or Swiss chard can be substituted for kale in this recipe.

DAIRY-FREE MAC & CHEESE

This dairy-free version of mac and cheese is creamy and luscious. We love using nutritional yeast, which is highly nutritious and easily found in powder or flakes at grocers. The yeast acts as the 'cheesy' component here. We also enjoy sprinkling it on popcorn or eggs!

If using spaghetti squash

PI
DF
V

Serves 4–6

450g brown rice, pasta or quinoa pasta (we like shells or elbows) or Baked Spaghetti Squash (page 126)

480ml full-fat canned coconut milk

150g nutritional yeast, plus more for sprinkling

Pinch of paprika, for colour

¼ teaspoon sea salt, plus more to taste

1. Cook the pasta as directed on the packet.

2. Meanwhile, in a saucepan over a medium heat, bring the canned coconut milk, nutritional yeast, paprika and salt to a rolling boil, then reduce the heat to low and simmer for 5 minutes, until all of the ingredients are incorporated and the sauce is creamy and smooth. Remove from the heat and set aside.

3. When the pasta is ready, drain and rinse it well. Add the pasta to the sauce, tossing to coat. Season with more salt, if needed and simmer the mac and cheese over a low heat for a further 2 minutes.

5. Sprinkle with additional nutritional yeast and serve immediately.

TIP
To make this a heartier main dish, we often add 340g cooked grass-fed minced beef or turkey for added protein.

Jennifer: When I want a comforting dish this is my 'go to'. I do not eat much dairy. For me, too much of it makes my nose stuffed up and slows my digestion. But when I have dairy only occasionally, my body digests it more easily. This dish fully satiates my cravings for creamy dairy every time.

BAKED MAC AND CHEESE WITH CAULIFLOWER

Because cauliflower is mild in flavour, this is a perfect way to sneak in some veg and added fibre for you and your kids: baking cauliflower with cheese and pasta is the perfect disguise. This recipe has been a family favourite for years. Here is our gluten-free version.

 If using spaghetti squash

Serves 4–6

280g brown rice, elbow macaroni or penne, or Baked Spaghetti Squash (page 126)

55g unsalted butter

3 tablespoons brown rice flour

2 tablespoons mustard powder

720ml milk

270g Cheddar cheese, shredded

250g cauliflower, chopped into small pieces and steamed for 5 minutes

35g Pecorino Romano cheese, grated

25g Gluten-free Breadcrumbs (page 99)

4 tablespoons crisp crumbled bacon (optional)

Sea salt

1. Preheat the oven to 180°C/gas mark 4.

2. Cook the pasta as directed on the packet. Drain and rinse it well. Toss in half of the butter and set the pasta aside.

3. Melt the remaining butter in a large pan over medium-low heat. Gradually add the flour and mustard, whisking constantly for about two minutes to make a roux.

Gradually add the milk, still whisking constantly, until a sauce forms, approximately 4 minutes. Add the Cheddar and whisk until it melts into the sauce.

4. Add the steamed cauliflower and stir to coat. Add the pasta and stir to cover with the cheese sauce and cauliflower. Season with salt.

5. Pour into a baking dish and top with the Pecorino, breadcrumbs and bacon if using. Bake for approximately 10 minutes, until it is hot and the top is golden brown and crisp.

6. Let rest for 5 minutes before serving.

TIP
You can play around with different cheeses, such as goat's cheese or Gruyère. You can also use other vegetables: We have made this with cooked winter or summer squash or broccoli in place of the cauliflower.

GLUTEN-FREE PIZZA DOUGH

There are a lot of gluten-free pizza dough recipes out there, but we believe our take on it is one of the easiest, tastiest and home-cook friendliest. Because of our Italian roots, pizza has always equalled celebration! We throw pizza parties with friends featuring this crust and lots of wine, and kid parties where each little one gets to create, eat and share their own pizza.

Makes two 30cm pizza bases

240ml warm filtered water (40°C to 43°C)

1 packet (7g) dried active yeast (about 1 ½ teaspoons)

2 tablespoons raw honey

2 tablespoons flaxseeds

4 tablespoons room temperature filtered water

120g tapioca flour

120g potato flour

210g brown rice flour, plus more for dusting

60g millet flour

1 tablespoon baking powder

2 teaspoons xanthan gum

1 teaspoon fine sea salt, plus more for seasoning

tablespoons extra virgin olive oil, plus extra for the pan and the top of pizza

¼ teaspoon apple cider vinegar

1. Grease two 30cm pizza pans and dust lightly with brown rice flour. Set aside.

2. In a small bowl, combine the warm water and yeast, mixing thoroughly. Add the honey and mix thoroughly. Let sit for 5–10 minutes, until the yeast mixture starts to foam.

3. Meanwhile, combine the flaxseeds and room temperature water together and set aside for 5 minutes.

4. In a large mixing bowl, whisk together the tapioca, potato, brown rice and millet flours, the baking powder, xanthan gum and salt. Add the reserved flaxseed mixture, olive oil and cider vinegar and mix. The pizza dough should be creamy and smooth with a consistency similar to cake batter.

6. Using a rubber spatula, divide the dough in half. Scoop each half onto the centre of a prepared pizza pan. Using wet hands, press down lightly and flatten the dough to create a thin, even, round pizza shell with slightly raised edges. (Keep wetting your hands to make this easier, and take your time to smooth out the dough.)

7. Preheat the oven to 200°C/gas mark 6. Put the pizza shells in a warm spot to rest and rise a bit, about 15 minutes.

8. When the oven is hot, bake the two pizzas, side by side on the centre rack, for 15 minutes or until golden. (If your oven is too small to accommodate both pans on one rack, use two racks, rotating the pans halfway through baking time to avoid overcooking on the lower rack).

9. Remove the baked pizza shells from the oven. Preheat the grill.

10. Brush the warm pizza shells with olive oil and season with salt. Top with your choice of sauce, cheese, cooked vegetables, fresh herbs, and/or meat. Drizzle olive oil all over the tops.

11. Grill the pizzas briefly to melt the cheese, 4–5 minutes. They are best served straight out of the grill.

TIP

If you only want one pizza, you can either halve the dough recipe or refrigerate half of the prepared dough for up to 2 days. Yeasted doughs do not freeze well because a deep freeze may kill the yeast. Even if we want just one pizza, we usually just make two and enjoy the leftovers, hot or cold.

GRAIN-FREE PIZZA DOUGH

This pizza dough may surprise you! It has an unusual list of ingredients and yet it bakes off beautifully. The crisp crust satisfies the Paleo person who is craving a pizza. It can also be used as a flatbread.

Makes one 30cm pizza crust

About half a head of cauliflower, outer leaves removed

1 medium egg

Pinch of sea salt

1 tablespoon dried oregano (optional)

120g plus 3 tablespoons tapioca flour

4 tablespoons extra virgin olive oil, plus more for drizzling

1 tablespoon warm filtered water

1. Preheat the oven to 200°C/gas mark 6.

2. In a food processor or by hand with a grater, shred the cauliflower until you have 5 tablespoons.

3. In a small covered saucepan over a medium-low heat, steam the cauliflower in about 4 tablespoons water until soft, approximately 6 minutes. Drain in a small, fine-mesh or nut strainer bag , squeezing out as much excess water as possible.

4. Whisk the egg in a mixing bowl. Add the cooked and drained cauliflower, pinch of salt, and oregano, if using, and mix to combine. Add the tapioca flour, mixing until thoroughly incorporated. Add the olive oil and warm water. Mix by hand to create a dough, then shape into a ball. The dough can be wrapped and frozen at this point or put in the fridge to be used within 2 days.

5. Place the ball of dough between two pieces of 23 × 27.5cm parchment paper. Flatten the ball with your hand. Using a rolling pin, roll out the dough to create a 30cm round. Slowly peel off the top piece of parchment paper. Carefully flip the remaining piece of parchment over so that your dough is on your pizza stone, pizza tin, or a baking sheet.

6. Top with your choice of sauce, cheese, cooked vegetables, fresh herbs and/or meat and bake for 15–18 minutes or until crust is golden brown. This pizza is best served straight out of the oven.

TIP
If you do not have parchment paper, wet the rolling pin with water to keep the dough from sticking to the pin. (It should be damp but not dripping.) You'll find the dough easier to roll out.

Get Your Boogie On

Exercise.

Our bodies are our temples. We live in them for our whole lives. If we keep them healthy and vibrant with exercise and a healthy diet, we feel alive, awake, present and empowered. Who doesn't want that?

Exercise doesn't have to be a drag. It doesn't have to last for hours on end to reap the benefits. What it takes is getting into your body and taking notice of how it feels. Listening to your body during exercise is a great way to do that. Here are a few tips to achieving a satisfying workout with powerful benefits.

Choose activities you enjoy: If you love to run, great. DO IT! If you feel dread every time you lace up your running shoes, by all means find something else. There are a million things you can do to get your heart rate up, so by golly, do something you enjoy! If you aren't sure what that is, take some classes and experiment. Think outside the box.

Change it up: It is good for your body to use different muscles, so mixing it up is not only beneficial and gets maximum results but will keep you from getting bored. Yoga one day, running the next, biking, dancing, hiking with a friend; whatever gets you excited on that particular day is what you should do. Listen to what your body wants and go with that.

Get outside: There is nothing like getting out in nature to get connected to our bodies. Not only does the outdoors tend to provide us with a more strenuous platform because of the variety of surfaces, but it also keeps things interesting. Rather than biking or running on something stationary and staring at the same thing the whole time, fresh air can revitalise us and reduce stress. Many of us stare at screens all day long, so it is beneficial to let nature be your exercise companion.

Pair up with a friend or a group: Having a hard time getting motivated? Exercise with friends! It is a great way to catch up. When you exercise with friends or a group, you hold each other accountable and you can be each other's cheerleader. For some people, signing up for group exercise activities is what gets them to stick to it. If that sounds like you, then look into local meet-up groups for activities or sign up for some classes. If you are a goal-oriented person, maybe a group race that has a training schedule leading up to the event will work for you. If that is what it takes, get going!

Commit: Even if you do just 30 minutes most days, you will feel the difference. Make getting a little exercise part of your daily routine and stick to it. Think of it as a gift to yourself, to your health, and to your vitality – and something that feeds every single aspect of your life. You deserve to feel amazing and exercise will absolutely help achieve that.

Take time to wind down, stretch and give gratitude: Exercise increases dopamine, serotonin and endorphins in your body – all natural feel-good enhancers. Just as beneficial as the workout is taking in some long deep breaths as you stretch and give gratitude for that beautiful body of yours that is strong and able.

It is in our nature to move. We weren't built to sit in front of computers all day. Our bodies need to release through movement, to stretch, and to work our muscles to remain healthy. Exercise affects brain health and the immune system, it oxygenates our cells and delivers a ton of other benefits. Boogie on with your fabulous self!

Jill: *Exercise is truly one of the highs of my life.* I love feeling into my body. I absolutely LOVE to dance. It works every part of my body and when the music is good I can really get into it, and feel my body unfurl. I make playlists of songs I love that are uplifting or go to dance classes with friends. I also have a running partner and road-biking partners, and we have a great time catching up on our lives while taking in the beautiful Colorado landscape.

And there is yoga practice. My sisters and I have been dedicated yogis for more than 20 years, and it is a daily practice for me. Some days it works with my breath and meditation, others it is anywhere from 15 minutes to an hour or more of flow. Whatever is needed to open and to feel present and alive. Yoga keeps my body strong and mind clear and focused. For me, morning time is where it is at. It is harder for me to commit after the day gets going, but if I set a time in the morning, then I make it happen. Exercise sets me up for the rest of the day. I feel energetic, clear and focused, as well as healthy, sexy and vibrant. I say, JUST DO IT. It will change your life to have a daily exercise routine. Satisfaction guaranteed! You are so worth it!

SMOOTHIES & BEVERAGES

There is no other way to say it – we are beverage junkies. At Shine we make our own award-winning beer as well as herbal potions. You can often find us sipping on one of these or a smoothie or cold-pressed juice. It is all about that continual party for the taste buds – that fix, that euphoric satisfaction that these unique beverages can deliver. Our smoothies are power-packed with nutrients, making them a great way to start the morning or for a pick-me-up in the afternoon. Some of these drinks are also fantastic mixers for your favourite spirits. We call it drinking mindfully!

'BE YOUR OWN MUSE.
YOU ARE BEAUTIFUL.'

NETTLE & MINT ICED TEA

Pt
DF
V

Makes three 240ml servings

720ml filtered water
3 tablespoons dried nettles (see Tip)
1 tablespoon dried peppermint
1 lemon
1-2 tablespoons raw honey

1. Bring the filtered water to the boil. Put the nettles and peppermint into a litre-size Kilner jar. Pour the boiling water over the herbs and stir in the honey. Cover and let it sit overnight at room temperature.

2. The next day, strain your tea into a jug full of ice. Let it sit for 30 minutes to allow some of the ice to melt.

3. Cut the lemon in half. Juice one half and pour the juice into the jug. Slice the other half.

4. Serve the tea over ice. Garnish each glass with a lemon slice.

TIP
Properly dried nettles will usually maintain their stinging sensation. If this is a concern, use kitchen gloves to handle the nettles. If you like, add lavender or dandelion leaf during the last 2–3 hours of steeping to increase the health benefits and vary the flavour.

Jessica: I made this tea often while I was pregnant and roasting hot in the height of summer. Not only is it extremely nourishing for both mama and baby, it is cooling and rejuvenating. Even if you are not pregnant, summer heat can be fun, but also irritating at times. Drink up!

WATER KEFIR

Makes 1 litre

1 litre filtered water, at room temperature

4 tablespoons unrefined sugar

⅛ teaspoon sea salt or ½ teaspoon molasses (optional: for added minerals)

5 tablespoons water kefir grains (please see Tip for purchasing instructions)

4 tablespoons fresh lemon or lime juice

1. Add half of the filtered water to a clean litre-size Kilner jar. Add the sugar and optional minerals, if using, and stir until the sugar dissolves. (Do not use metal utensils for stirring because they react and leach metals which can harm the grains.) Gently stir in the water kefir grains. Top the jar off with the rest of the filtered water.

2. Cover the jar with a cloth or cheesecloth and seal by securing the cloth with an elastic band. Place the jar in a dark cupboard at room temperature for 48 hours to ferment.

3. When ready, strain out the grains using a plastic or silicone strainer (do not use metal as it can damage the grains). Stir in the lemon juice.

4. The kefir is ready to drink. Enjoy it in the morning or throughout the day to aid digestion. Or you may leave it on the countertop for several days before drinking it. The flavours will blend and the kefir will continue to ferment and become slightly carbonated.

TIP

Water kefir grains are better to use than a water kefir culture powdered starter, since the powdered version does not have as many strains of bacteria and cannot be reused. Please ensure that you choose water kefir grains, not milk kefir grains! Room temperature water works best. Do not use honey instead of sugar, since honey is antibacterial and can be hard on the culture. You can retain one-third of your water kefir grains from your first batch to begin a new batch. While your water kefir is fermenting, you should see the grains floating, growing in size, and multiplying. For more information, visit www.culturesforhealth.com.

BEETROOT KVASS

Kvass is a traditional Eastern European medicinal tonic with an earthy, salty taste that's very cleansing for the liver and beneficial for healthy digestion. You can drink it or use it in place of vinegar in salad dressings. We really enjoy sipping this before or after meals, served chilled in a wine glass.

Makes about 2 litres

3 medium beetroots, peels on
1 tablespoon sea salt
About 2 litres filtered water

1. Wash the beetroots to remove the dirt. (Be careful not to scrub too hard; you want the beneficial bacteria to remain, as it is a crucial part of the fermentation process.)

2. Chop the beetroots into medium pieces and place them in a clean 2-litre Kilner jar. Add the sea salt and fill the jar with filtered water, ensuring that you leave 1cm of headspace. Tightly screw on the lid, turn the jar upside down, and give it a light shake to incorporate the ingredients.

3. Let the beverage ferment at room temperature, on your countertop, for approximately 2 weeks (see Tip). Taste it: If it has a deep earthy, pickle-like flavour, it's ready. It could take a few days longer, depending on the temperature of your kitchen.

4. When the flavour of the kvass is how you like it, store it in the fridge for up to 1 month. It is great as a digestif or really any time of day. There is no need to strain out the beetroots. You can even eat them as they get poured out into your glass.

TIP
Make sure to 'burp' your jar every day for the first 3 or 4 days of the fermentation process to let the gas escape. Do this by removing the jar lid for a couple of seconds and then securely twisting it back on. If it's available, the best way to make beetroot kvass is with raw grass-fed whey (rather than the water and salt). Whey is the watery part of raw milk that remains after the formation of curds. It reduces the fermentation time and adds a sour flavour to kvass.

WATERMELON COOLER

Watermelon seeds are very nourishing for the kidneys, which can get taxed during long, high-energy summer days, and are rich in minerals and great for healthy hair and skin. We recommend blending them right in with the rest of the watermelon. Watermelons with seeds tend to be more flavourful.

Makes about two
300ml servings

300g bite-size pieces of
ripe watermelon

720ml full-fat canned coconut milk

8 ice cubes

Place all of the ingredients in a blender and blend for approximately 2 minutes, until cool and creamy. Serve immediately.

TIP
If you don't have coconut milk in the house, you can substitute filtered water or coconut water for a frothy watermelon beverage, served neat.

Jennifer: *I love watermelon and I love coconut milk,* so having them together as a beverage is deeply satisfying. I often drink this at the end of the day, in the late-summer sun, while swinging in my hammock. Watermelon is mostly made of water, so it is a very cooling and hydrating to the body.

SUMMER LOVIN' ELIXIR

Chill out in the heat of summer with the cooling power of cucumbers, lime and mint. Blended together with a burst of healthy leafy greens and more, this drink is the ultimate refresher.

Makes about two
300ml servings

1 small cucumber, peeled

Flesh of ½ avocado

2 teaspoons fresh lime juice

2 teaspoons fresh mint leaves

60g greens of your choice,
(spinach, beetroot greens,
Swiss chard or kale), chopped
and lightly steamed (see Tip)

240ml filtered water (see Tip)

16 ice cubes

Put all of the ingredients in a blender and blend for approximately 2 minutes, until smooth. Serve immediately.

TIP
Lightly steaming the greens makes them easier to digest and all of the nutrients more readily available. Coconut water can be exchanged for the filtered water for added electrolytes and sweetness.

GOLDEN ANTI-INFLAMMATORY SMOOTHIE

Turmeric is revered around the world as one of the most powerful anti-inflammatory foods. However, its highly beneficial compounds can be hard to absorb without the presence of fat or black pepper. We know it sounds strange to include black pepper in a smoothie, but the flavour is masked and the benefits of doing so are worth it. This drink is truly so good for you and tastes amazing as well.

Makes about two
300ml servings

2 teaspoons chia seeds

480ml full-fat canned coconut milk

2 tablespoons powdered turmeric

¼ teaspoon freshly ground
black pepper

2 teaspoons raw cacao powder

½ teaspoon fresh ginger,
finely chopped

350-400g frozen mango
or frozen banana

2 tablespoons coconut oil

2 tablespoons raw honey

16 ice cubes

Soak the chia seeds in the coconut milk in the blender for approximately 10 minutes (see Tip). Add the remaining ingredients to the blender and blend for approximately 1 minute, until smooth. Serve immediately.

TIP
Soaking the chia seeds in liquid before blending enhances the digestibility of the seeds.

'PRESSED' GREEN JUICE

PI
DF
V

Makes 2 servings

½ bunch spring greens
½ bunch curly kale
2 sticks celery or ½ cucumber
480ml filtered water
  or coconut water
½ bunch parsley
Handful of baby spinach
Nut-milk strainer bag

1. Chop the spring greens, kale and celery or cucumber into small pieces. Put them in a high-powered blender, add the filtered or coconut water and blend for 30 seconds. Add the parsley and spinach and blend until you have a rich green purée.

2. Pour the purée through the nut strainer placed over a bowl. Strain the juice, using your hands to push all the liquid out from the pulp. (Discard the pulp.)

3. Drink your juice, enjoying all of the amazing benefits!

TIP

This juice can be made in advance and kept in the fridge for up to 24 hours. Make sure to shake it before drinking, as it will separate. Lightly steaming the greens makes them easier to digest and all of the nutrients more readily available.

Jennifer: *I love to have my daily green juice in the morning…* I use a nut-milk strainer bag to separate the pulp from the liquid. The bag is made of mesh material, which is super durable and may be used over and over again. I stick to all green vegetables to keep the sugar content low and my blood sugar balanced. Even though I eat a lot of other vegetables daily, this juice provides me with my essential morning boost.

CHERRY ON TOP SMOOTHIE

PI
DF
V

Cherries and bananas are great for muscle recovery after a big workout, while the greens and avocado supply an antioxidant boost. This beverage is fun for the whole family!

Makes about two
300ml servings

Flesh of ½ avocado (see Tip)

1 banana

200g frozen pitted cherries

60g greens of your choice (spinach, beetroot greens, Swiss chard, or kale), chopped and lightly steamed (see Tip on page 157)

¼ teaspoon ground cinnamon

2 tablespoons raw cacao powder

1 teaspoon raw honey

240ml milk of your choice (whole milk, almond milk or rice milk)

16 ice cubes

Place all of the ingredients in a blender and blend for approximately 2 minutes, until well-blended and smooth. Serve immediately.

TIP
We tend to use the avocados that have been in the fridge for a day or two for smoothies and open new ones for salads and sauces.

MAGIC
MONKEY

This smoothie has the peanut butter cup flavour that we loved
as kids. It is a good-for-you treat that is a powerful energiser
post-workout or as a midday snack.

Makes about two
300ml servings

3 dates
1 ½ bananas
360ml milk of your choice (whole
milk, almond milk or rice milk)
2 tablespoons sunflower
or almond butter (see Tip)
1 tablespoon raw cacao powder
2 teaspoons raw honey
2 teaspoons spirulina
24 ice cubes

Put all of the ingredients in a blender and blend for approximately
2 minutes, until smooth, but still thick. Serve immediately.

TIP
You can substitute cashew, macadamia,
or peanut butter as the nut butter.

Jessica: *Raw honey, especially honey that is local* to where
you live, is a very healing food. It is rich in live enzymes, which are
beneficial for digestion, and it is very energising. I experimented on
my child (who loves honey) by giving her 2 teaspoons of raw local
honey every morning to build her immune system and to help with the
seasonal allergies she typically gets in the springtime. She no longer
gets allergies from pollen and her immune health is strong. Having the
raw honey every day, which is rich in local pollen, gave her small doses
of the pollen so her body became used to it.

DAILY DOSE
SMOOTHIE

This vitamin-packed smoothie is a great way to get your daily dose before you even walk out the door. It includes plenty of high-energy foods, rich in antioxidants and protein. Raw eggs are extremely healthful, but it is important to use eggs from a sanitary source: That means choosing free-range, organic eggs from pastured chickens whenever possible to avoid unwanted bacteria. The yolk of the egg has the most vitamins, minerals and good fats.

PI
DF
V

Makes two 300ml servings

2 lightly soft-boiled free range eggs (boiled for about 1 minute)

120g greens (spinach, beetroot greens, Swiss chard or kale), chopped and lightly steamed (see Tip on page 157)

225g frozen berries of your choice

Flesh of ½ avocado

120ml milk of your choice (whole milk, almond milk or rice milk)

16 ice cubes

Combine all of the ingredients in a blender and blend for approximately 2 minutes, until smooth, but still thick. Serve immediately.

TIP
We believe in using just the yolks in the smoothie because they are more easily digested, much higher in nutritional value than the whites and are much lower in possible allergens.

ROOT TO RISE COFFEE

Putting fat such as ghee and coconut milk or cream into your coffee helps to metabolise the caffeine more slowly, keeping you from getting jittery and then crashing. It also assists in brain function and boosts energy. Enjoy the buzzzzzzz.

PI
V

Makes about two 300ml mugs

480ml freshly brewed coffee

120ml full-fat canned coconut milk or grass-fed cream

2 heaped tablespoons raw cacao powder

2 tablespoons grass-fed ghee

1. Add all of the ingredients to the blender and blend, starting on low and gradually increasing to high, for a total of about 30 seconds.

2. Serve hot and frothy from the blender.

TIP

This coffee is wonderful as is, but it's also delicious served with about ½ tablespoon of honey, maple syrup, or your favourite unprocessed sweetener.

Fat Is Fabulous

We are big BIG advocates for good fats. It is one of the foundational building blocks in our diets. It helps maintain our energy and keeps our brainpower in tiptop shape. Healthy fats help build cell walls and make it easier for nutrients to get into our system. Our brains are made up of about 60% fat, so eating good fats helps with brain function, too. Fats also help regulate blood sugar and stabilise our metabolisms so we feel satiated and avoid that constant tug to run to the fridge or larder for high-carb, high-salt or sugary snacks.

When we say good fats, we mean luscious, nourishing, cell-building, heart-healthy fats like olive oil and coconut oil, not processed ones like corn, soy, rapeseed or safflower fats. Including healthy fats in your diet can actually help you shed weight and keep you feeling energised and alert. It is the good stuff. And to really reap the benefits of the good stuff, it is also important to simultaneously cut down on processed sugars and refined carbs.

Below we provide an overview of our favourite fats, which we use throughout the book, along with best uses for each. More stable fats with higher smoke temperatures are better for cooking, while some of the others are best used in vinaigrettes and to drizzle on finished dishes for added flavour and nutritional value. Smoke temperature is the point at which an oil literally starts to smoke when overheated. As it smokes, it loses its nutritional value and can even release toxins; it also can impart a burnt or 'off' flavour to the food you are preparing.

Extra-virgin olive oil: EVOO is an excellent oil for vinaigrettes and as a finishing oil. You can cook with extra virgin olive oil, too, as it is more stable than a lot of other oils. However, it does start to lose valuable nutritional elements at higher temperatures, so choose another fat for high-temperature cooking. EVOO is high in antioxidants and can help reduce inflammation in the body.

Coconut oil: This is a healthy unsaturated fat to use when roasting, sautéing, frying and baking. Unrefined coconut oil is better to use than refined, because it is in its 'pure' form, meaning it has more nutritional value and is not processed in any way. It is also more stable at higher temperatures. Keep in mind that it does have more of a coconut flavour than refined versions. Coconut oil can aid in weight loss, boost the immune system, assist with proper digestion and regulate the metabolism.

Toasted and untoasted sesame oil: These are great oils for finishing sauces, dressings and sautéing. Untoasted sesame oil is a good choice for stir-fries and sautés, while toasted sesame oil is better for drizzling, as it has a strong flavour and thus should be used sparingly. These oils are very high in linoleic acid, which is one of the two essential fatty acids that our bodies cannot produce. This fatty acid is necessary for healthy blood, arteries and nerves. It can also help our skin and other tissues stay youthful by preventing dryness.

Ghee/Clarified Butter: Ghee is an excellent option when frying, sautéing, roasting and baking. Ghee is butter with the milk solids removed. This is done to enhance the butter flavour and makes it more stable for cooking over heat. It also enhances the health benefits. Ghee can help heal your digestive tract, balance your cholesterol levels and increase your energy level. It is a staple in Ayurvedic and Indian cooking. We love to make our own (for recipe, see page 30).

'LIFE IS CHANGE. CHANGE IS LIFE. NOTHING STAYS THE SAME. EVENTUALLY EVERYTHING WE HOLD ON TO MUST BE LET GO. TRUST AND ACCEPTANCE ARE OUR GUIDES AND LOVE IS THE WAY.'

'YOU ARE THE CREATOR OF YOUR OWN EXPERIENCE.'

SWEETS & TREATS

We'd be hard-pressed to find someone who is not a sweets person. The real challenge is that often sweets are processed and refined, which makes them unhealthy. But if you use nutrient-rich wholefood ingredients like raw cacao powder, almond flour, coconut oil, pumpkin purée and raw honey, sweets can be good for you. Our recipes are not only delicious, but also nutritious and they will satisfy. Our theory is to indulge, not deprive! You can have it all, even when it comes to dessert.

Jessica: *I have thought a lot about how to help my kids have a healthy relationship* with sweets, since, like all kids, they are hard-wired to love them. I want my kids to enjoy sweets and indulge occasionally, but not feel like that is all they want or crave. One of the ways I attempt to forge this healthy relationship is to have them start the day with something savoury as opposed to sweet. I have noticed that on days when I give them a sweet breakfast, they crave more sweets throughout the day. I also started them early in their lives on things like raw sauerkrauts, stock, grass-fed minced meats, eggs from pastured chickens, ghee and wholesome vegetables. (I'm telling you, start them young, or introduce these things slowly, and it is possible!)

Another one of my goals is to not to offer sweets to them at home unless it's a healthy kind of sweet such as our homemade ice lollies or jelly (pages 174 and 175). They will be offered plenty of sugary treats while they are out in the world, so I let them get it outside the home. I also decided not to reward my kids with sweets because it can send a message that sweets are fun and good while other foods are not. I believe we as parents have a huge influence on how our kids relate to sweets and food in general. It is a good reminder for me to check in on my own relationship with food.

The Skinny on Sweets

We all have a relationship with sweets. For some of us, they feel like a naughty indulgence. We may even feel dependent on them for happiness or satisfaction and want more as soon as the sugar rush is gone.

Sweets are tricky that way. Sugar is hidden in many processed foods, which is just one more reason why we are big advocates for a wholefood lifestyle. Sugar acts like a drug and can be addictive, releasing dopamine in the body to give us a sugar high, and then, when it wears off, sending us into withdrawal and wanting more. Excess sugar depletes our nervous system and immune system, increases inflammation in the body and contributes to weight gain by building resistance to certain hormones that regulate the metabolism.

Cutting out processed sugars will absolutely single-handedly improve your health. But we get it – sweets are feel-good food for many of us, so we are here to talk to you about how to satisfy that sweet tooth in a way that actually satiates your body. You can create a relationship with sweets that is satisfying, good for you and empowering. Here are a few of our favourite alternative sweeteners.

Local raw honey has not been heat-treated or processed, so all of the powerful enzymes, vitamins and minerals are intact. It has antibacterial properties and can help strengthen the immune system. It can also be great for allergies: if taken before the allergy season starts, local honey can build up immunities to certain pollens because the honey contains small amounts of pollen from the local environment.

Coconut sugar is made from the sap of the coconut palm that has been extracted, boiled, dehydrated and granulated. It has a rich flavour almost like brown sugar.

Pure maple syrup contains important antioxidants and minerals. The darker and richer in colour and flavour, the more nutritional value it has. Make sure to choose pure maple syrup or it will most likely have refined sugar added.

Each of these sweeteners metabolise in your system more slowly and are more stabilising than processed sugars. But even so, it is still sensible to use them in moderation because eating sweets – even these healthier alternatives – can sometimes make you crave more sweets.

When you experience a craving for a sweet treat, here are a few quick snacks that will give you immediate satisfaction without making your blood sugar go crazy:

Frozen grapes: Throw a bag of grapes in the freezer to munch on when you want a sweet snack. They have tons of antioxidants and help with digestion and hydration, too.

Watermelon with coconut cream: You know the cream that sits at the top of a can of coconut milk? We like to skim it off the top and mix it with some watermelon or berries for a delicious treat. To make it separate more easily, refrigerate a can of coconut milk – the cream will rise to the top.

A bowl of frozen berries topped with your favourite milk: The frozen berries may cause the milk to get slushy (depending on the milk you choose), but slushy or not, grab a spoon and satisfy that sweet tooth.

Warm milk or boiled water with raw cacao powder: When you want a cup of hot chocolate, try this combination instead and, if you so desire, add a touch of one of the alternative sweeteners listed above or a drop of peppermint oil or both. This drink is warming and will help quench your thirst for chocolate. (If you want to avoid any caffeine stimulation, substitute carob powder for the raw cacao.)

Slices of apple or banana with unsweetened almond or other nut butter and local raw honey: This combination gives you energy-producing protein on top of quelling your sugar craving.

A few squares of dark chocolate: It contains a ton of antioxidants and is a great quick fix. Make sure to look for a cacao content of 70 per cent or higher since this will ensure lower sugar and more antioxidants. To up the ante, smear on some nut butter.

RAW CHEESECAKE WITH CHERRY SAUCE

We have vivid memories of Mum making cheesecake throughout our childhood. She always let us put the biscuits in a bag and take turns with the rolling pin to crumble them for the crust. She would top this cake with a sweet cherry sauce that was unforgettable. This is a raw version of our favourite dessert made by Mum.

Makes one 23cm cake

CRUST:

130g raw almonds

75g pitted dates
(approximately 4–5 Medjool)

40g raw coconut flakes

½ teaspoon vanilla extract
(to make your own, see opposite)

Small pinch of sea salt

FILLING:

360g raw cashews, soaked in warm
water for at least 2 hours

180ml fresh lemon juice
(from about 3 lemons)

160g raw honey

180ml coconut oil

1 tablespoon vanilla extract

Small pinch of sea salt

Fresh Cherry Sauce (recipe opposite)

1. To make the crust: put the almonds in a food processor and run until the almonds are finely ground. Add the dates, coconut flakes, vanilla extract and salt and process until thoroughly combined. The mixture should stick between your fingers when squeezed. Remove from the food processor and form into a ball.

2. Put the ball of dough in an ungreased 23cm springform tin or pie tin (see Tip). Press the ball of dough into the tin, working it up the sides, until the crust is 6mm thick throughout and covers the bottom and sides evenly.

3. To make the filling: rinse and drain the cashews. Transfer to a clean food processor, add the lemon juice, honey, coconut oil, vanilla extract and salt. Purée until the filling is silky smooth, approximately 90 seconds.

4. Pour the filling into the crust, smoothing the top with a spatula. Put the cheesecake in the freezer for at least 1 hour to set. (The cheesecake can be made up to 3 days ahead.)

5. If you're using a springform tin, remove the sides of the pan before serving. Top the whole cheesecake or slices of the cake with the cherry sauce.

TIP

We find this recipe works best in a springform tin, but it can be made in a normal pie tin as well. You may have a little bit of extra cashew filling if using a pie tin. We love drizzling this over fresh fruit, fruit salad or toast.

FRESH CHERRY SAUCE

Makes about 240ml

225g fresh or frozen pitted cherries
2 tablespoons coconut oil
2 teaspoons maple syrup

1. In a blender, combine 150g of the cherries with the coconut oil and maple syrup and blend until smooth. (Add a touch of water to keep things moving if necessary, but use as little as possible; the sauce should be thick.)

2. Chop the remaining 75g cherries and put them into a small mixing bowl.

3. Stir the cherry purée into the chopped cherries. Chill for at least 10 minutes before serving. The sauce can be made up to 1 week ahead and refrigerated in an airtight container.

GLUTEN-FREE VANILLA EXTRACT

Makes 720ml

9 vanilla pods
1 × 750-ml bottle of gluten-free vodka, such as potato or grape vodka

1. Using a sharp paring knife, cut each vanilla pod lengthways in half, leaving 2.5cm at one end connected. Add the vanilla pods directly to the bottle of vodka and replace the cap tightly.

3. Store in a cool, dark place for 3–4 months, giving the bottle a shake every once in a while.

4. After this time period, your vanilla extract is ready for use. No need to strain out the vanilla pods. The extract will last for years in your larder.

TIP
Gluten-free vanilla extract is hard to find in shops and can be expensive. This may seem like a lot of vanilla extract, but it has a long shelf life and is a quick, easy and less expensive way to make it yourself. If you want to make less, use 3 vanilla pods per 240ml of vodka. Store in a glass bottle with a tight-fitting lid.

MY KID'S FAVOURITE ICE LOLLIES

Makes six 115g ice lollies or four 170g ice lollies

280g fresh or frozen organic strawberries or blueberries or a combination

2 tablespoons raw honey

340g natural yogurt or full-fat canned coconut milk

½ tablespoon vanilla extract (to make your own, see page 171)

1. Purée the berries in a high-powered blender or food processor. Add 1 tablespoon of the honey to the berry purée and blend until combined.

2. In a small bowl, stir together the yogurt or coconut milk, vanilla extract and remaining tablespoon of honey until combined thoroughly.

3. Pour 1–2 tablespoons of the berry purée into each lolly mould. Spoon in 1–2 tablespoons of the yogurt mixture on top. Alternate between the berry purée and yogurt mixture for a layered effect until the moulds are full.

4. Freeze the lollies for at least 6 hours before serving (see Tip). They will keep in the freezer for at least 2 months.

TIP
Your ice lollies should be completely frozen before serving. To help release the frozen lollies from their moulds, run the bottom of the moulds under warm water for about 30 seconds.

Jessica: These ice lollies are a staple in our freezer year-round. They are simple and delicious, and I like that this recipe has so few ingredients, which makes it easy on the body, as opposed to shop-bought brands that usually contain many different ingredients and preservatives.

FROZEN FUDGE ICE LOLLIES

Shop-bought chocolate fudge ice lollies (we call them Fudge Pops in the US) are usually loaded with refined sugar and preservatives. This is our good-for-you version. This treat incorporates many healing foods – each ingredient is powerful in its own right – while satisfying your chocolate craving on a hot day.

Makes six 115g ice lollies
or four 170g ice lollies

2 × 400ml tins full-fat coconut milk

1 ½ teaspoons vanilla extract
(to make your own, see page 171)

3 ½ tablespoons raw honey

60g raw cacao powder (or carob
powder if you would like a
caffeine-free alternative)

1 ½ tablespoons (13g sachet)
grass-fed powdered beef gelatine

1. In a small saucepan over a medium heat, warm the coconut milk until nearly boiling. Whisk in the vanilla extract and honey. Reduce the heat to a simmer. Whisk in the cacao powder until thoroughly combined. Turn the heat off.

2. Sprinkle the gelatine over the surface of the coconut milk mixture. Let it sit for 3–4 minutes to allow it to activate, then whisk the gelatine into the milk mixture until all the lumps are gone. Remove the pan from the hob and allow it to cool for 20–30 minutes.

3. Pour the cooled coconut milk mixture into the ice lolly moulds (see Tip), dividing it evenly. Freeze the ice lollies completely before serving. They will be ready in 6–8 hours.

TIP

If you don't have ice lolly moulds, small paper cups can be used instead. Fill them 2.5–5cm from the top of the cup with the cooled coconut milk mixture and let it freeze long enough to hold the lolly sticks upright, about 45 minutes. Insert the sticks, fill the cups completely and return to the freezer. When fully frozen, peel away the paper from the lollies and enjoy.

GOOD FOR YOU JELLY

PI
DF

Makes one 20cm baking dish

1 ½ tablespoons (13g sachet) grass-fed powdered beef gelatine

120ml cool filtered water

20ml hot (almost boiling) filtered water

360ml white grape juice

120ml cranberry juice (see Tip)

140g fresh strawberries, sliced

1. Put the gelatine in a large bowl. Add the cool water and whisk vigorously until the gelatine thickens. Add the hot water and stir to mix; the mixture will thin out a bit. Add the grape and cranberry juices and mix well.

2. Put the strawberries in a 20cm square glass baking dish. Pour the gelatine mixture over the berries and stir gently.

3. Cover the dish with clingfilm and put it in the fridge until firm, at least 3 hours or overnight.

4. Cut into cubes, scoop it with a melon baller or use biscuit cutters to make cute shapes for serving.

TIP
You can definitely play with the types of juices used in this recipe. I have, on occasion, even used freshly juiced juices.

Jessica: My daughter's five-year-old friend always says this tastes like gummy bears. Little does she know the nutrients I sneak in! Grass-fed gelatine is a surprising superfood. Gelatine works from the inside out to help strengthen hair and nails and give skin a healthy glow, as well as improving the health of joints, ligaments and tendons.

BANANA CHOCOLATE MOUSSE

Carob powder and raw cacao powder can be used interchangeably in this recipe. Carob is a chocolate alternative, for people who don't do caffeine or stimulants – or don't want caffeine before bedtime. It is a pulse that doesn't taste exactly like chocolate but has a similar flavour. Raw cacao is chocolate in its purest form and it is Paleo friendly. This mousse is great topped with berries, nuts, coconut flakes, etc. Kids love this healthy dessert!

Serves 4–6

10 dates, pitted and soaked in water for 2-3 hours

1 ripe banana, peeled and roughly sliced

3 ripe avocados, stoned, flesh scooped out of shells

120ml maple syrup

4 tablespoons raw honey (local if possible)

60g raw cacao powder or carob powder

2 teaspoons vanilla extract (to make your own, see page 171)

Put the drained dates in a food processor and process for 1 minute. (The dates will form a ball. This is fine.) Add the banana and avocado and process for another minute. Add the maple syrup, honey, cacao powder and vanilla extract and process for a further minute. Chill the mousse in the fridge for at least 1 hour before serving. Stored in an airtight container, it will keep in the fridge for up to 3 days.

TIP
This can also be used as a healthy vegan chocolate icing or whipped cream for cakes, cupcakes and ice cream.

RAW CHOCOLATE TRUFFLES

We are lucky enough to enjoy these truffles almost daily. They are always on the menu at the restaurant and they are our sweet treat after meals. It is fun to experiment with flavours – we sometimes even add medicinal herbs and spices. These are very satisfying because even though a single truffle makes just a small dessert, they have the perfect amount of sweetness to satisfy any sweet tooth.

Makes 10 truffles

130g whole raw almonds
4 tablespoons coconut oil
4 tablespoons raw honey
90g raw cacao powder
2 teaspoons sea salt

1. Put the almonds in a food processor and blend until they almost form a butter, about 2–3 minutes. Transfer to a large bowl.

2. Warm the coconut oil to a pourable consistency. Pour the oil into the ground almonds, add the honey, cacao powder and salt and mix well.

3. Spread the truffle mixture into a small baking tin or food storage container, cover with clingfilm and put in the fridge to cool until it hardens, at least 6 hours or overnight.

4. Using a tablespoon or melon baller, scoop about 2 tablespoons of the truffle mixture at a time and roll it with your hands into small balls. Arrange the truffles on a serving plate and serve immediately.

TIP

There are many variations on these truffles you can make. For example, for our Cherry Vanilla Truffles we add 2 tablespoons chopped dried cherries and 2 teaspoons vanilla extract to the truffle base. Let your imagination and your taste buds be your guide.

RAW CHOCOLATE CHIP COOKIE DOUGH

One of our earliest cooking memories is of the three of us climbing atop chairs to reach the counter to help our mum make chocolate chip cookies. The combination of brown sugar, butter and vanilla extract with chocolate chips made licking the bowl and spoon so unbelievably heavenly – though there is nothing that causes ear-piercing screaming like trying to share two batter-filled beaters between three little girls! And we definitely sneaked some dough while mum wasn't looking, so that experience very often ended in a tummy ache! This is our version that is reminiscent of that experience, but much easier on the belly. Enjoy the dough on its own with a spoon or as a spread on fruit such as apples, bananas and pears.

Makes about 435g

225g raw tahini (sesame seed paste)
125g raw honey
3 tablespoons coconut oil
1 teaspoon vanilla extract
(to make your own, see page 171)
Tiny pinch of sea salt
40g cacao or carob chips

Put the tahini, honey, coconut oil, vanilla extract and salt in a food processor and process for 1 minute. Pour the 'batter' into a small bowl and stir in the chips. Cover and refrigerate for up to 5 days.

TIP
To make a healthier version of cookie dough ice cream, add this to softened home-made vanilla ice cream, straight out of the ice cream maker.

CHOCOLATE CHIP PALEO COOKIES

PI
DF
V

Makes 20 cookies

250g almond flour
½ teaspoon sea salt
½ teaspoon bicarbonate of soda
120ml melted coconut oil, plus more for greasing
120ml maple syrup
2 teaspoons vanilla extract (to make your own, see page 171)
170g dark chocolate chips

1. Mix together the almond flour, salt and bicarbonate of soda in a large bowl.

2. Blend together the coconut oil, maple syrup and vanilla extract in a small bowl.

3. Pour the wet ingredients into the dry ingredients and mix together well. Stir in the chocolate chips and let the dough chill for at least 1 hour in the fridge (see Tip).

4. When you're ready to bake the cookies, preheat the oven to 180°C/gas mark 4. Line a baking sheet with parchment paper or grease it with coconut oil.

5. Scoop approximately eight balls of dough, each about 1 tablespoon in size, onto the prepared baking sheet. (Do not crowd the pan.) Bake for approximately 10 minutes, until lightly golden and then transfer the cookies to a wire rack. Repeat with the remaining cookie dough.

6. Serve warm or store in an airtight container for up to 5 days.

Jill: It is a joy to bake these cookies for my nieces or for friends because they are easy to make, ready in no time and I always get a lot of love for them. Friends that can't do dairy or who are Paleo go nuts for them, and people are always surprised at how good they are for you. They have excellent flavour and texture, plus the almond flour makes them high in protein and a high-energy snack or dessert.

TIP
You can also make the dough ahead of time and freeze it, wrapped in a double layer of clingfilm. Thaw it in the fridge overnight before baking.

GRAIN-FREE PUMPKIN BREAD

Makes a 23 × 12.5cm loaf

1 tablespoon coconut oil,
plus more for greasing
230g almond butter
115g pumpkin purée
1 ripe banana, mashed
4 tablespoons maple syrup
2 medium eggs, whisked
20g coconut flour
2 teaspoons ground cinnamon
½ teaspoon ground nutmeg
½ teaspoon bicarbonate of soda
½ teaspoon baking powder
Pinch of sea salt

1. Preheat the oven to 180°C/gas mark 4. Grease the loaf tin with coconut oil (see Tip).

2. In a large bowl, mix together the almond butter, pumpkin, banana, maple syrup, coconut oil and eggs.

3. In a small bowl, mix together the coconut flour, cinnamon, nutmeg, bicarbonate of soda, baking powder and salt.

4. Add the dry ingredients to the wet ingredients and mix until combined.

5. Pour the batter into the prepared loaf tin and bake for 45–50 minutes, until a toothpick or sharp knife inserted into the middle of the loaf comes out clean.

6. Cool the loaf in the tin for about 30 minutes before removing from the tin and slicing and serving. Wrapped in clingfilm, leftovers will keep for up to 3 days.

TIP
If you don't have the right size loaf tin, you can use a bigger one and do a shorter baking time. Do not use a smaller loaf tin because the ingredients may rise and overflow, creating a big mess! This recipe can also be made in a 23cm square baking tin, but reduce the baking time to about 40 minutes.

Jessica: *This is a great grain-free snack or accompaniment to breakfast.* My daughter loves when I pack it as a treat with her lunch. We like it smothered with ghee and local raw honey.

DECADENT GRAIN-FREE BEETROOT BROWNIES

Makes one 23cm square tin

4 medium beetroots (about 450g) to make 240ml beetroot purée

2 tablespoons extra virgin olive oil

4 tablespoons apple juice or water

4 tablespoons coconut oil, plus 1 tablespoon for greasing the pan

180g raw cacao powder

100g ground almonds

230g almond butter

210g raw honey

120ml maple syrup

1 ½ tablespoons vanilla extract (to make your own, see page 171)

2 teaspoons baking powder

¼ teaspoon sea salt

1. Preheat the oven to 190°C/gas mark 5.

2. Remove the roots and stems from each beetroot and scrub them under water to remove any dirt. Put the beetroots on a large piece of aluminium foil. Drizzle with the olive oil, wrap up the beetroots, and roast them for 1 hour to 1 hour 15 minutes, until they can be easily pierced with a knife. Remove the beetroots from the oven to cool and reduce the oven temperature to 160°C/gas mark 3.

3. When the beetroots are cool, remove the skins by rubbing each beetroot with kitchen paper or a tea towel. The skins should come off easily (although they will stain the towel). Slice the beetroots into medium-size pieces. Put them into a blender or food processor with the apple juice and purée until smooth. Measure 240ml of beetroot purée for the brownies (see Tip).

4. Melt 4 tablespoons of the coconut oil and pour it into a large mixing bowl. Add the cacao powder, ground almonds, almond butter, honey, maple syrup, vanilla extract and salt. Mix well with a wooden spoon until the ingredients are completely incorporated.

5. Grease a 23cm square baking tin with the remaining 1 tablespoon coconut oil. Pour the brownie batter into the prepared tin and bake for approximately 50 minutes. The brownies are done when a skewer or toothpick inserted into the centre comes out mostly clean.

6. Let the brownies cool for 20 minutes before slicing and serving. Transfer the brownies to an airtight container for storage. They keep well at room temperature for up to 4 days.

TIP

If you have more than four beetroots in the bunch and want to roast them all, roasted beetroots are excellent sliced and tossed in red wine vinegar or orange juice. Serve them hot or cold in salads or as a side.

Nestled at the formidable foot of an ancient rocky mountain in the heart of Boulder, Colorado, lies an enchanted gathering place known as Shine. Shine was created by the Blissful Sisters in 2012 as a place for people to congregate, celebrate, transform and heal. It is a place to connect people to their hearts though nourishing food, hand-crafted potions, award-winning house-brewed beer, community gatherings and a beautiful team to serve them.

Connect to your heart.
SHINE from within.

With love,

The Blissful Sisters

INDEX

THANK YOU

To our editor Jessica Goodman, for being able to hear our individual voices from the start, yet keeping us moving in a direction together. And for always seeing the lotus blossoming out of the mud.

To our publisher Kyle Cathie, for seeing us and believing that this book would be something that needed to be shared.

To Shadi Ramey, our diligent fearless recipe tester that met our crazy for getting the job done in an unbelievably short amount of time.

To Eva Kolenko, the bad-ass passionate photographer who captured our creations so eloquently.

To Jeffrey Larson, our talented food stylist who took such care and pride in his work to bring our recipes to life.

To Anja Schmidt for being the spark.

To Mark Latter, thank you for interpreting our vision from over the pond.

To Kate Bailey our PR Goddess and dear friend, we are so grateful for your constant support and insight.

To The Golden Hoof, for allowing us to use your beautiful farm for our author shots and for being such an inspiration to so many for the way you live and farm.

To Chantel Pierret, founder of Emerging Women, for that pivotal brainstorming session that was an invitation to step into our power and Own It.

A shout out to our big Jersey Italian Family who are wild and full of life and love. They taught us from a very young age to think outside the box and go after our dreams. That it is not about whether you win or lose but about how you play the game with love and laughter always prevailing.

To our parents Maureen and Dennis Emich who always helped light up our path and nurtured our creative spirit. Their love and support has been our foundation from which to leap.

To our brother Dennis who has a heart of gold and has taught us patience, compassion and how love really does conquer all.

Jessica: To my husband, Marek, thank you for teaching me so much about love and partnership. Your kindness, patience and acceptance never cease to amaze me. I feel so blessed to be in this together. To my beautiful girls, Sofie and Amelie, you continue to inspire me to be the absolute best version of myself. Thank you for bringing so much silliness and joy, for teaching me so much and of course humbling me. You light me up every single day.

Jennifer: To my hubby Eck who loves me for exactly who I am. Thank you for supporting me to do whatever makes me happy. I feel beyond blessed to share this lifetime with you. And to my nieces, you brighten my every day.

Jill: To my sisters, my soul mates, I am so happy we chose to walk this path together. To my nieces, you remind me of my playful spirit and of how big we can love. To all the loves in my life that have helped shape all that I am and all that I will continue to grow to be. I offer my humble gratitude.

To our staff and our community that have supported our individual selves, our restaurants and our wild harebrained ideas over the years.

From the heart,

The Blissful Sisters

Jessica Emich is the first born and the alpha of the three. She was the first to get married and have kids as well as the first to get in the business. She graduated from University of Nevada Las Vegas with a Hotel & Restaurant Management degree as well as attending the California Culinary Academy in San Francisco. Jessica was the co-owner and Executive Chef at her restaurant Trilogy Wine Bar and Lounge and has since received a Masters Degree in Holistic Nutrition as well as a certification in Metabolic Typing. She is the co-owner and mastermind behind the menu at Shine Restaurant and Gathering Place. She joins her passion for food and health to create a unique menu of nourishing comfort food. She resides in Boulder, CO with her beautiful daughters and husband.

Jill Emich is the middle of the three sisters and a bit of a closet dancing queen. She graduated from the University of Nevada Las Vegas with a degree in Hotel & Restaurant Management and attended the California Culinary Academy in San Francisco. She was the owner, music talent buyer and bar manager of the Blissful Sisters' first restaurant Trilogy Wine Bar and Lounge. Her mission is to help people tap into their magic and power within as conscious creators. She is currently the co-owner of Shine Restaurant and Gathering Place, Shine Potions™ and Shine Brewing Co™. Her focus is on product development, event production, community outreach and beer and potion connoisseurship. She loves to connect with others and to be of service to the greater good. Through her role at Shine, she encourages people to dance, play, explore and dig deeper into their personal beings, to share their gifts and SHINE from the heart. She lives in her quiet little cabin in Boulder, CO.

Jennifer Emich is the youngest of the three, yet the most even-keeled. She graduated from the University of Nevada Las Vegas with a degree in Elementary Education, which has helped her work with all sorts of people (and their inner child). She co-owned Trilogy Wine Bar and Lounge where she ran the front of house and business operations. She is currently the co-owner of Shine Restaurant and Gathering Place and Shine potions™ and Shine Brewing Co™. She is a great listener and enjoys connecting with the guests and getting to know what makes them smile (and coming back) as well as the day to day operations. She lives in Boulder, CO with her husband and their beloved cat Willow.